Indian Ethos and Culture in Nissim Ezekiel's Poetry
A Critical Study

Sandeep K. Thorat

ATLANTIC
PUBLISHERS & DISTRIBUTORS (P) LTD

Published by
ATLANTIC
PUBLISHERS & DISTRIBUTORS (P) LTD
7/22, Ansari Road, Darya Ganj, New Delhi-110002
Phones : +91-11-40775252, 23273880, 23275880, 23280451
Fax : +91-11-23285873
Web : www.atlanticbooks.com
E-mail : orders@atlanticbooks.com

Branch Office
5, Nallathambi Street, Wallajah Road, Chennai-600002
Phones : +91-44-64611085, 32413319
E-mail : chennai@atlanticbooks.com

Printed in India at Nice Printing Press, A-33/3A, Site-IV, Industrial Area, Sahibabad, Ghaziabad, U.P.

Dedicated to

My uncle Late Dr. H. T. THORAT,
Ex-Director, GVISH, Amravati.

Preface

The poetry of Nissim Ezekiel seems to be unexplored with reference to Indian ethos and culture. It is difficult to find a critic who has exclusively been made efforts to discuss Ezekiel's poetry coming in terms of India and its origin, religions, society and its attitudes, problems, poverty, superstitious practices, blind beliefs, happiness and sufferings, etc. in context of Indian ethos and culture. As his poetry continues to be prescribed in University and College syllabi, there seems to be no discontinuity to Ezekiel's critical horizon.

Though Ezekiel seeks continuous flow in his poetry, the present book attempts to find a gradual growth of mature thought towards spirituality and religious aspects from his early poetry to the recent. In the beginning, there is an impact of his immature youth and consequently he composed poetry on the themes like love and sex. An image of a pagan woman predominates his early poetry. On the other hand, his recent poetry reveals influence of his maturity as a man of full experience of all ups and downs of life. His recent poetry expresses the themes like spirituality and religious-philosophical strains. It appears that in his recent poetry he seems to be more philosophical on life and human concerns.

The first chapter of the book, however, attempts to study Indian ethos and culture in brief with the motive of investigating its reflection in Ezekiel' poetry. The second chapter comprises Ezekiel's life, works, initiation and development as a poetic genius. The third chapter explores briefly Indian ethos and culture in contemporary Indian English poetry of some of the major poets. The fourth chapter gives the critical analysis of some of the major early poems of Ezekiel on Indian ethos and culture. In this chapter, an attempt is made to analyze Ezekiel's early poetry from critical point of view to form and confirm a view on his poetry. The fifth chapter analyses the reflection of Indian ethos and culture in poetry written in his recent phase of life. And the last chapter of the book is the conclusion.

Ezekiel really seems to be true representative of Indian society as his themes of poetry are chosen from almost all walks of life. The aim behind selecting the poet for the present study is to discuss the reflection of continuous quest for self and Indian cultural ethos in his poetry. He deals with his own experience through themes like superstitions, blind beliefs, urban India, man-woman relationship, love and sex, illusion with religion and spirituality, and the disillusionment. Making life happy without breaking old morals and values is a striking feature of Ezekiel's poetry. Being modern, the poet feels dissatisfied with the existing morals, and social and religious values. Though, he wrote poetry satirically on domestic quarrels, he was dissatisfied with the depicted codes and conducts of married life.

Indeed, the book provides better opportunities to readers regarding Indian ethos and culture. In fact, it attempts to highlight social, political, and religious aspects of life and, therefore, is of universal importance to everyone.

Sandeep K. Thorat

Acknowledgements

I take the opportunity to acknowledge my gratefulness to Dr. K. S. Khandare, my Ph. D. supervisor, who always encouraged me to go through this unforgettable experience. The blessings of Dr. A. L. Kulat, the Chairman, Board of Studies in English, Sant Gadge Baba Amravati University, also inspired me to accomplish this task. I am grateful to Dr. P. R. Rajput, Principal, Staff Members, and Students of S. S. S. K. R. Innani Mahavidyalaya, Karanja Lad for their direct and indirect support.

I could not forget the blessings of my parents Shri. K. T. Thorat and Smt. Shakuntalabai. I acknowledge the support of my wife Mrs. Pratibha to motivate me to take up this project. My daughter Miss. Sharvari and my son Ishant have equally helped me a lot.

I am equally thankful to Mr. Harjeet Singh, Publication Co-ordinator of Atlantic Publishers & Distributors Pvt. Ltd., New Delhi, India for making it possible to bring out this book in a short time.

Sandeep K. Thorat

Contents

1 Introduction

In the present chapter, an attempt has been made to elaborate Indian ethos and culture in order to investigate its shades in Nissim Ezekiel's poetry. At the same time efforts have been made to study India and its origin, religions, society and its attitudes, problems, poverty, superstitious practices, blind beliefs, happiness and sufferings, etc. in order to percolate its ethos and culture in Ezekiel's poetry. The emergence of Ezekiel as an Indian poet writing in English is equally a part of study in the present chapter of the book. Finally a brief estimate is made to find out the shades of Indian ethos and culture in Ezekiel's poetry.

The term, ethos and culture, need to be briefly explained, though both entities appear inseparable. The word 'ethos,' in general, means the moral ideas and attitudes that belong to the particular group or society. "Ethos is a Greek word, meaning "character" that is used to describe the guiding beliefs or ideals that characterizes a community, nation, or ideology" ("Wikipedia"). "The characteristic spirit, disposition, or tendency of a people or community regarded as an endowment and as expressed in their customs" (Webster 436). Ethos is a discipline that examines one's morality or the moral standard of the society. It is derived from culture. It works to maintain holistic atmosphere and welfare in community.

> Indian ethos is based on the two Universal Truths, every Indian believes in God or the Supreme Power and everything must be in interconnected at a deeper level. The

basic unity of life cannot be broken. Love and sacrifice therefore emerge as the only means for a meaningful living. Based on this holistic vision, Indians have to develop the work ethos of life, where they feel all work, physical or mental, managerial or administrative, has to be directed towards a single purpose. Divinity of a human being is not merely a notion but a truth that can be experienced in the stillness of the mind. The individual or 'self' is the central focus in Indian ethos. The divine element in the individual is only a portion of the universal or cosmic consciousness. It lays great emphasis on values. It is based on Indian scriptures that provide eternal knowledge. It is a belief that all work is worthy and honourable. It equally emphasizes on duties and responsibilities. Indian ethos follows the dictum Vasudhaiva Kutumbakam: to consider the whole world as one's own family. (Define Ethos_bms.co.in.html)

The word Culture is derived from the Latin *cultura* stemming from '*colere*,' meaning "to cultivate". Culture, in general, means the customs and beliefs, art, way of life and social organization of a particular country or group. Culture means: "Enlightenment or civilization. The sum total of the attainments and activities of any specific period, race, or people, including their implements, handicrafts, agriculture, economics, music, art, religious beliefs, traditions, language and story" (Webster 314).

Culture generally refers to pattern of human activities, a state of intellectual development or manners. The influence of social, economical, political, religious, and psychological forces on the development of an individual may be summed as culture. The culture is a system of continuous changes because of situations, and circumstances. Cultural ideas may be transferred from one society to another. The human beings always seek modification in cultural values. But rich values in a person remain unchanged because they are deep-rooted in his heart:

> Indian culture is rich and diverse and as a result unique in its very own way. Its manners, the way of communicating with one another, etc. are one of the important components of Indian culture. Even though we have accepted modern means of living, improved our life styles, our values and beliefs still remain unchanged. A person can change his way of clothing, eating and living but the rich values in a person always remains unchanged because they are deeply rooted within his heart, mind, body and soul which we receive from our culture. People from centuries have been influenced by culture. (Wesley and Chandra 2)

Ethos determines culture or cultured behavior:

> Every country has its own culture and character based on the social, political, and economical environment in which it operates. From that culture spring forth the national ethos, which prescribes a code of conduct for its citizens and creates the context for ethics and values in that society. Indian ethos and wisdom a legacy and heritage from its hoary past envisaged a socialistic pattern of society, with an accent on redistributions. It has always been a champion of renunciation and rectitude, rather than accumulation and aggrandizement. (Devarajan 34)

The above discussion reveals that both the words ethos and culture are strictly related and depend on each other. It can be said that ethos and culture are the two sides of the same coin. Both words in the context of India as a society appear inseparable. Therefore, Indian ethos and culture, the term unifies a single whole. On the other hand, separating Indian ethos from Indian culture create no effects to the full expectation. The present research treats both the terms together as they appear inseparable in their effects to a little extent.

To elaborate Indian ethos and culture, it becomes imperative to know India. It is difficult to explain what India is in a straightforward way to some extent, but an attempt can be made to understand it. India is a land of great heritage, culture and religion having the river Ganges originating from the great mountain Himalayas flowing toward the Bay of Bengal. It is India where even a river can be compared with mother who teaches her sons lessons of civilization. *Ganga Maa* (Mother Ganga) has been flowing continuously for thousands of years along with a stream of culture.

India has a great history of Haddappa and Mohenjo-Daro, the great ancient cities existed before thousands years, taught *Sindhu Sanskriti* to Indians which can be traced as the beginning of Indian culture to a little extent. It is a land of Vedas, Puranas and Upanishadas which is the fruit of joint efforts of our Rishi and Muni who placed a platform and code of conduct in life. Because of the ways shown by these Rishi and Muni, the Indians can feel peace of mind, a sacred truth of life. T.S. Eliot, a great poet also referred the Indian words *Shanti, Shanti, Shanti,* in his poem "The Waste Land". It shows that there is no better place in the world to feel peace of mind than India. In this respect Roman Rolland is quoted by Jawaharlal Nehru as he says, "If there is one place on the face of the earth where all the dreams of living men have found a home from the very earliest days when man began the dream of existence, it is India" (Nehru 89).

The noteworthy thing is that the way of life shown by Rishi and Muni in Vedas, Puranas and Upanishadas and which traces the root of Indian culture has been followed by Indians. It is this culture which makes the land sacred and pious in giving the peace of mind to Indians and even to the others. In shaping Indian ethos and culture, the contribution of Indian religion cannot be overlooked from its formation. The culture has been continuously flowing with new streams because of the religious influence on Indian mind; we can easily call it Hinduism. Swami Vivekananda, in his speech delivered at Chicago, referred "Hinduism is the mother of all religions." He represented Hinduism as flexible as any otherism. Hinduism has several threads to accept and tolerate every one of any creed, caste and religion. It will not be wrong to say that Hinduism is the culmination of Indian ethos and culture.

Hinduism does not work as a religion but a civilization, a parameter to mould Indian way of life. Hinduism is:

> extremely comprehensive. It has not only a religious, but also a social meaning, for the caste system is a very important constituent of it. As the name of a religion, it excludes those religious societies which do not recognize the Veda as authoritative-Buddhism, Jainism etc.—but includes practically all other shades of Indian religion from the first centuries B.C. down to the present day. (Clemen 108)

In fact, the state of realizing our relationship with all through union with God was considered in India to be the ultimate end and fulfillment of humanity. To say, that the end of life is spiritual fulfillment and it can be achieved by the path of truth. The truth is the base of Hinduism, less a religion in the Western sense of the word than a fellowship of all those who accept the immutable laws of right conduct and fashion.

Buddhism, another remarkable religion, influenced Indian way of life. It showed a middle path between the life household and the ascetic life of social withdrawal. Buddhism concentrated on the solution of sufferings in life: "The Buddha wished to concentrate on the two most important questions about existence: How can we minimize suffering, both our own and that of others? And how can we attain inner peace?" (Molloy 108).

Jainism did not spread in India widely due to its noble ideals and provoking thoughts. Its quality of strong acceptance of non-violence seemed to be uncompromising. Sikhism proved the best religion of essential quality of India. It mostly grew in Punjab. Though there was a big gulf between ideology of Hindu and Muslim, efforts had been made to bridge division and misunderstanding.

Indian caste system plays an important role in understanding Indian ethos and culture. The arrival of Aryans into India created racial and political problems, while the existing race, the Dravidians, had a long support of civilization. A division of superiority separated them from each other. Then there were also backward tribes, nomads or forest dwellers. The conflict among these races grew caste system. Life was graded as *Shudras* or laborers and unskilled workers; *Vaishyas,* the merchants; *Kshatriyas,* or rulers and warriors; and *Brahmins*, priests and thinkers. "In the Hindu hierarchical social structure based on the age-old institution called *Chaturvarnya,* that is, the four-tiered social system first propounded in Manusmriti, the ancient Hindu code of laws" (Murugan 5).

Though these grades appear outdated due to the social adjustment among people, caste enabled more peaceful solution in smooth working of Indian life. In this connection, Molloy refers The Bhagvad Gita to understand the caste system of India and says that "active people will perfect themselves through the unselfishness of their work; and intellectual people will perfect themselves through teaching and study" (71). In this context Nehru asserted,

> The Aryans not only graded the society into four castes, but also divided individual's life into four stages: *Dharma,* the first stage of growth and learning period of life; *Arth,* the second one of the household; *Kaam,* the third one that of an elder statesman; *Moksh*, the last stage of the recluse. (86)

Another remarkable influence on Indian psyche is that of Islam. It has greatly influenced the shades of 'Hinduism'. The Hindu started to adopt Islam. But this impact lasted for a certain period:

> The majority were originally Hindus who, owing to political events which culminated in the dynasty of the Mohammedan Mogul emperors, adopted Islam, some by compulsion and some voluntarily. Of course this great

> extension of the foreign religion was bound to have effects on the faith of the Hindus, although, these were confined to certain period and certain men or groups of men. Even after the Mohammedan domination of India had ceased, however, the religious differences between Hindus and Mohammedans continued to play a large part in the life of India. The British Government has exploited them to the utmost. (Clemen 94)

It seemed that there was a harmony among Hindus and Muslims as most of the converted Muslims were earlier Hindus:

> Hindus and Muslims in India developed numerous common traits, habits and ways of living and artistic tastes, especially in northern India—in music, painting, architecture, food, clothes, and common traditions. They lived peacefully as one people, joined each other's festivals and celebrations, spoke the same language, lived in more or less the same way, and faced identical economical problems. (Nehru 268)

It is Islam to introduce the concept of monotheism and brotherhood in India after Upanishads. But after some time, caste system changed the picture and it itself become the victim of Manusmriti. Later on, Islam had lost its grip in domestic life, in the fashion of dress, in the ways of cooking, in the marriage ceremony and in the etiquette of Rajput, Maratha and Sikh Princes.

The canvas of India is seen influenced by various movements. One of the remarkable influences on Indian life is of *Bhakti Movement* which rose due to the human brotherhood of Islam in South India and later spread in the North. It affected the ways of life of both the Hindus and the Muslims. It rejected the rules of Manusmriti and gave equal status to all men and women. It shook the very fabric of Indian society for more than two centuries. During British rule, modern scientific thought resulted into two movements. One was *Brahma Samaj* led by Raja Ram Mohan Roy. It taught secularism and socialism. While another *Arya Samaj* led by Swami Dayanand. It percolated Brahmanism and gave rise to *Hindu Mahasabha* which traces the culmination of *Rashtriya Swayamsewak Sangh*. These movements have shaped new ways of thoughts and feelings in the minds of the Indians. It resulted in the fact that Indians devoted for their languages and culture:

> Many European and Indian scholars delved deep into the past and produced original works as well as translations of Sanskrit classics to show that the Indian culture was not inferior to that of any other country. Thus, contrary to the expectations of the British imperialists, patriotic sentiments and progressive ideas began to stir in Indian minds and, in course of time, they influenced the literature, philosophy and political thought of India. (Khan 43)

The foreign influences changed the very fabric of Indian religion. These changes differed greatly in kind and degree. The two great religions Islam and Christianity influenced India from political point of view. But Islam put far less influence than did Christianity. Christianity succeeds in changing the Indian psyche:

> European values have gradually posed a major challenge to traditional Hinduism.... The most significant European influence on India, however, was English.... Although India became independent of Britain in 1947, British influence is evident in modern India's law, education, architecture, rail transportation, and military life. (Molloy 90)

However, Indian canvas is so large to acquire the influences of foreign religions. The founder fathers of this great independent nation accepted the multi-religious form of its society in order to make India a secular land. The Independent India did not want to form a Government based only on the faith of the Hindu majority. Despite religious differences, modern Indian secular state demands to make a society which can give remarkable scope to the total population of the nation. Though India is influenced by outside world from every angle, whatever an Indian produces becomes essentially India. Thus India shapes itself as an independent nation where religious practices, cultural reform are obviously seen. The people of all religion in India practice tradition, superstitions, and cultural, societal and religious activities. These activities of people of various race and religion help to reflect Indian ethos and culture.

The spiritual tradition of making '*guru*' (a teacher) in one's life, especially in Hinduism, is praiseworthy. Making *guru* and devotion to *guru* is an old custom of Indian spirituality. The word '*guru*' means the person who removes darkness from one's life. A true *guru* shows spiritual path to his disciple. This is a concrete example of Indian ethos and culture.

It has been a common feature of Indian ethos and culture to treat woman equal in every walks of life. A woman has been playing an important role in shaping the dignity of India. But the Aryans did not find it essential as their culture was thoroughly patriarchal. Today, the situation has changed and a woman has been given every right almost equal to man in each and every field.

In India, there is a tradition of believing in God and Saint as a part of *Bhakti Movement*. In this adventure, people believe in God and Saints as their own religions allow. They want peace of mind. Sometimes, it is believed that faith in God makes their way of life easy without difficulties and problems. The people try to seek presence of God in temple, mosque, gurudwara, and church. They pray and worship God by offering flowers and fruits.

The most important belief of Indians is rooted in superstitious practices. These include going to witches instead of doctor for ailment on the diseases; crossing a road by a black cat; seeing a face of a widow; chanting a name of God on biting of a snake or a scorpion; cawing of a crow foretells the arrival of some guest; custom of child-marriage, etc. These blind beliefs and attitudes of people reveal Indian ethos and culture. It is arresting of religions to show kindness to animals. A devout Hindu does not kill or eat animals. "Cows often wander along Indian streets, and cars and taxis take care to drive around them. Furthermore, visitors to some Hindu temples may find monkeys and even mice well fed and running free" (Molloy 85).

Indian tradition treats guests as Gods and takes them as their family members. A special care of guest is taken; they are never left hungry, even if there is no food to eat. There is a famous proverb in Sanskrit, "*Atithi devo Bhava*". Respect for elder is a main component of Indian ethos and culture. This mode of giving respect to elders is natural and not forced. It springs from the inner core of the individual. Sometimes, blessings are taken from elders by touching their feet. In short, Indian ethos and culture is a base of intellectual development or manners. The social, religious, and political influences build the growth of a human being.

However, the above discussion emphasizes a fact that India has been leading itself toward building a nation and flourishing since past centuries out of numerous influences starting from the arrival of the Aryans and their ways of life. But it is accepted view that Hinduism has been running through Indian ethos and culture like blood in the vein throughout the ages. The teaching of the classics like Vedas, Upanishads, Bhagvad Gita, and Mahabharata is inseparable from Indian psyche. The Islam and the British helped to shape and re-shape Indian ethos and culture beyond imagination. India, because of the strength of its origin, has been able to maintain its identity and dignity in the world.

It is interesting to note that the writing on Indian ethos and culture appeared in Indian languages in ancient times. But the native people brought about a change in their art and social organizational customs, beliefs and attitudes. As a result of it, they began to write in English language to which they were not natives. They made efforts to follow the language of other culture and also got success. They not only followed the western language, but also maintained a beautiful combination of choosing the Indian scenes for writing in English language. In fact, this is an arresting example of Indian ethos and culture. However, they formed a particular group in India. Therefore, it seems compulsory to trace the beginning of such great Indian writers writing in English.

Ample of literary forms have already been handled by writers writing in Indian languages. However, the British rule brought English Language in India and it percolated in Indian society. The Anglicization of Indians began during the British rule in India and Indians mostly influenced by English Language. It flourished at the hands of different writers who wrote in various forms such as novels, dramas, short stories, and poetry. Many Indians tried their best in composing poetry in English language. These poets insisted to give a separate national identity to their literature. Hence they coined some terms like Indo-Anglian, Indo-English, Indian English, Indian literature/writing/fiction/drama/poetry.

Generally, in the history of Indo-Anglian poetry, Henry Louis Vivan Derozio is considered as the first Indian poet writing in English. Then there is a long list of Indian poets. The growth of Indian poetry in English seems to have taken a significant turn when Lord Macaulay introduced the education of English language in India. By the time, Indians had gradually begun to speak, think, and write in English. In this regard the Bengali critic and poet Buddhadeva Bose has put it: "The best of Indian-English verse belong to the nineteenth century, when Indians came nearest to speaking, thinking, and dreaming in English" (Lal 5).

The year 1947 tries to classify Indo-Anglian poetry into two phases—pre-Independence and post-Independence. The great poetic talents proved their ability in pre-Independence era like Michael Madhusudan Dutt (1824-1873), Toru Dutt (1856-1897), Manmohan Ghose (1867-1924), Sri Aurobindo Ghose (1872-1949), Puran Singh (1881-1931),

Rabindranath Tagore (1861-1941), Sarojini Naidu (1879-1949) etc. However, their poetry is rooted in the quagmire of imitation and tradition. It may be resulted out of their newly introduction to English language and literature. Tagore's formal poems in English discover pleasure in the world of senses and his sensibility was idealistic and romantic. One can easily find out root of Tagore's *Gitanjali*, though written with great poetic talent, in mysticism and saint tradition of India. As David Cevent has expressed that the accomplishment of new Indian poetry has been one of liberation from Tagore and his "long sentimental imitation of Shelley and Kalidasa" (qtd. in Harrex 145).

On the contrary, there was a remarkable change in Indo-Anglian poetry in the post-Independence era. The era was an intellectual escape from hope and aspiration of the earlier period. The post-Independence poets marked their poetry with rationalism, realism, modernism and a passion to explore the meaning of existence through everyday life. They preferred a poetry written in a clear, hard, unsentimental tone, and in everyday language. They sought frankness, meaning, and order in personal relationship into their poetry. They found relief in describing sex with its harsh reality, the city with its dirty, poverty-stricken and degenerate humanizing environs. Thus, the post-Independence poets opened a new chapter with genuine enthusiasm in Indo-Anglian poetry. As Bruce King observes:

> Modern Indian English Language poetry is one of the many 'new literatures' which began to emerge at the end of the Second World War after the end of colonialism. Unlike the creative writing of Africa and the Caribbean, modern Indian Poetry in English has been neglected by most critics, foreign readers and intellectuals for it has no obvious direct relationship to the cultural movements which led to national independence; by 1947 the situation had changed and with it the concern of the new poets became their relationship to and alienation from the

> realities of their society. In particular they faced a challenge from older nationalist intellectuals and from regionalists who demanded a renaissance of the culture of the pre-colonial languages of India. (1)

In the post-Independence era, Nissim Ezekiel, Dom Moraes, P. Lal, Adil Jussawalla, A.K. Ramanujan, R. Parthasarthy, Gieve Patel, A.K. Mehrotra, Pritish Nandy, Keki Daruwalla, Shiv K. Kumar, Jayanta Mahapatra, Arun Kolhatkar, Kamala Das, Monika Varma, Gauri Deshpande and many more contributed to the Indo-Anglian poetry. These poets tried to capture the very Indian ethos, culture, spirit, attitude, situations from real life in their poetry:

> Cultural bewilderment, identity crisis, perplexity, introspection, rejection of old spiritual and religious values are the dominant themes in the contemporary Indian poetic scene. The rich contribution of the 'new poets' in an alien language but nonetheless an original idiom, has made a tremendous impact in the arena of Indo-Anglian poetry. Nissim Ezekiel was one of the renowned poets belonging to the post-Independence era of Indian Writing in English, who contributed immensely through his poetic endeavors. Ezekiel enriched Indian English poetry through his modernist innovations and techniques, bringing forth themes associated with a wider range of concerns and interest. (Khanna 592)

The 'new poets' created the language for poetry, they did not manipulate it. Their works are marked with originality, both in theme and diction. The feelings of reality, freshness and craftsmanship impart excellence to their works. In this sense K.R.S. Iyengar remarks:

> The Western influences are still there, but even more than the 'Content', it is the manner of expression which involves both the choice of language and the flow of rhythm that is being adjusted and attuned to the temper of the new age. Hopkins, Yeats, Eliot, Auden, Dylan Thomas, perhaps also Allen Tate and Wallace Stevens,

> have taught our poets, the importance of taking their art seriously. They have realized that easy writing cannot make good poetry. Neither mere imitation nor wanton angularity, neither frantic incoherence nor fabricated obscurity can make words live or sing themselves out. The profession of poetry is a concentrated endeavour and an exacting discipline. It is to the credit of the 'new poets' that they are prepared to take their vocation seriously. (649)

However, Nissim Ezekiel is a typical name for composing poetry on themes suitable to Indian culture and its ethos. He is an Indian poet to the core writing in English. He occupies a unique position among Indo-Anglian poets of post-Independence era. He is honoured with Padmashri and Sahitya Akademi Awards for literature. As a modern poet, he rejects the past. It is quite suggestive from the title of his first book of poems *A Time to Change* (1952). He opposes the idealism and romanticism of the earlier and tries to reflect Indian ethos and culture peeping into a typical Indian situation with an alienated insight. "After the death of Sir Aurobindo, Nissim Ezekiel is the first major voice that represents, more or less, the change of an era" (Daruwalla 56) in the history of Indian English Poetry.

Ezekiel has sustained quality of verse to Indian English Poetry. He is recognized as a major poet in the history of Indian English Poetry. Almost every critic in and outside has taken special care of Ezekiel's poetry because of its unique characteristics. "His respect for craft makes his poetry much more than a mere fulsome expression of an emotion or an idea" (Abidi 287). Ezekiel could achieve these characteristics to his poetry because of his Indianness. It was his close relations with Indian environment that endowed a rare significance to his poetry:

> Nissim Ezekiel is a Jew and his relationship with the country of his adoption is so fundamentally deep that he represents a dimension of Indianness which others who

> claim an 'umbilical connection' with the country find so natural to articulate in an altogether different manner. His Indianness is a condition of the mind, the product of intellectual and emotional sympathy without a trace of self-consciousness, a kind of identification which may more adequately be termed as spiritual kinship. (Abidi 287)

In his poetry, Ezekiel has pointed out the typical Indian issues such as man-woman relationship, traditions, superstitions, blind beliefs, familiar relationship, religio-philosophic strain and use of so-called *Babu Angrezi* etc. As far as the use of language is concerned Ezekiel deliberately made use of present continuous tense which is a characteristic Indian attitude of the users of English language.

Ezekiel's poem "Night of the Scorpion" emphasizes superstitious and traditional-bound ethos of Indians. Perhaps, his aim is to show how the whole community is deeply rooted in old belief that cannot be severed by social reforms. In another poem "The Visitor," Ezekiel very skillfully highlighted the blind belief that followed by the Indian community. "Background, casually" is a poem in which caste-bound attitude of Indians is exploited. Ezekiel is ill-treated by the Muslims, the Hindus, and the Christians in a Roman Catholic School. He also voices the poverty-stricken attitudes of Indians through the poems like "The Truth about the Floods," "The Railway Clerk," "Entertainment," etc.

While developing man-woman relationship, Ezekiel expresses the ethos of an Indian woman performing various roles such as daughter, mother, wife and object of sex in poems such as "Poem of the Separation," "Morning Walk," "Motives," "Marriage," "Servant," "In India," "The Couple," "Haiku". These poems contribute an opinion that "his poetry has acted as a mirror for reflecting life as it is actually lived in this backward place" (Karnani 105).

Ezekiel does not spare even Indian modern *Sadhus* in expressing their break up from Indian ethos and culture. In the poem 'Guru', Ezekiel attacks the hypocritical attitude of Indian modern *Sadhus* and faith of Indians who worship them blindly. Speaking about these *Sadhus*, Ezekiel reveals their indecisive attitude and hopelessness. Such *Sadhus* are responsible for the degradation of cultural ethos.

Another striking feature of Ezekiel's poetry is his employment of *'Babu Angrezi'* or 'Pidgin English' to depict characteristic Indian attitude. He uses irony, humour and satire as weapons of depicting Indian ethos and culture. He endeavors to demonstrate it mostly in his *Very Indian Poem in Indian English*. There was no Indian poet to take risk to treat such topic in poetry. Joseph Furtado tried to use Pidgin English in poetry:

> No one has, to the same extent, taken comparable risks in verse. And the first poet to try—and this was in the 1920s—was Joseph Furtado (1872-1947). He wrote some poems in pidgin or bazaar English, like 'The Fortune-teller' and 'Lakshmi'. But, Furtado himself did not use Pidgin English extensively, except in a few humorous poems. He was interested in it as a source of humour. He seemed to have been unaware of the possibility of its developing into a creole. A pidgin, in any case, arises under the pressure of practical circumstances in a bilingual situation. (Parthasarathy 7)

Nevertheless, Nissim Ezekiel made a successful experiment of using pidgin or bazaar English in Indo-Anglian poetry. It is felt that Ezekiel excels among his contemporaries not only in describing Indian situations, but also in using irony, humour and satire as weapons of depicting characteristic Indian attitude by employing *Babu Angrezi* or "Pidgin English".

However, Ezekiel's observation of Indian society is praiseworthy to bring forth the typical Indian ethos and culture through different Indian situations:

> Ezekiel observes the ordinary events of the common man at a distance that helps him to treat the weakness of the society with a touch of irony. In this process he

> gets the opportunity to discuss the superstitions in the society, the community feeling among the villagers, the blind belief and stories associated with it and above all, certain typical Indian emotions. (Pandey 12)

The basic platform of his poetry is strong because of his interest in reflecting himself and the life around him. In fact, poetry for him seems to be a record of personal pursuit of self-discovery in which his psyche tries to dive deep in the water of Indian ethos and culture. But it is his psyche, which brings out his social concerns, his social ideal, and his genuine sympathy for suffering humanity.

Ezekiel constantly moves between two points—quest for personal identity and concern for the people. This was always to remain the central theme of his poetry. This theme also runs through his early collection of poems *A Time to Change*. Michael Garman rightly remarks that in this poem, "the poet's religion sympathetically assumes a double aspect—the introspective contemplative and the outward-active" (212). Chetan Karnani finds his poetry as a "first-hand record of life's growth" (168). For V.A. Shahane Ezekiel's poetry seeks "a balance between an existential involvement with life and an intellectual quest for commitment" (254). Ezekiel like T.S. Eliot and other modern poets also believes that "all art is based on the conflict and contrast of opposites".

Indeed, Ezekiel treated poetry as a way of life, as a continuous flow and as something, which is inextricably related to existence. He expresses in his foreword to *Sixty Poems*: "poetry is elusive; to write a poem is comparatively easy". Because of it, his all the five collection and his subsequent poems find relation to one another and form one organic whole. An early poem throws light on a latter one because for him poetry is a constant flow like life itself. This concept of poetry really makes us to reach his intriguing voice:

> A poem is an episode, completed
> In an hour or two, but poetry

Is something more. It is the why
The how, the what, the flow
From which a poem comes,
In which the savage and the singular
Are all dissolved; the residuce
Is what you read, as a poem, the rest
Flows and is poetry. (*CP* 13)

Though Ezekiel seeks continuous flow in his poetry, the present investigation attempts to find a gradual growth of mature thought towards spirituality and religious aspects from his early poetry to the recent. In the beginning, there is an impact of his immature youth and consequently he composed poetry on the themes like love and sex. An image of a pagan woman predominates his early poetry. On the other hand, his recent poetry reveals influence of his maturity as a man of full experience of all ups and downs of life. His recent poetry expresses the themes like spirituality and religious-philosophical strains. It appears that in his recent poetry he seems to be more philosophical on life and human concerns.

It is on this basis, the present investigation makes efforts to study his early poetry and recent poetry separately. The present investigation studies his poetry into two phases—the early phase and the recent one. His early phase of poetry includes volumes: *Early Poems* (1945), *A Time to Change* (1952), *Sixty Poems* (1953), *The Third* (1959), *The Unfinished Man* (1960), *The Exact Name* (1965), while his recent phase of verse includes *Poster Poems* (1969), *Hymns in Darkness* (1976), *Latter-Day Psalms* (1982), and the Latest Poems in *Collected Poems* (1989).

The topic of the present study seems to be apt and suitable in the context of Indian ethos and culture as reflected in Nissim Ezekiel's poetry in order to bring about a reform in religious and social practices in India. Therefore, the selection of the topic and the poet is of great significance. Secondly, the work of Nissim Ezekiel seems unexplored with reference to Indian ethos and culture. So, the poet is selected for the present study.

The first chapter of the book, however, attempts to study Indian ethos and culture in brief with the motive of investigating its reflection in Ezekiel's poetry. Chapter second comprises Ezekiel's life, works, initiation and development as a poetic genius. The third chapter explores briefly Indian ethos and culture in contemporary Indian English poetry of some of the major poets. The fourth chapter gives the critical analysis of some of the major early poems of Ezekiel on Indian ethos and culture. In this chapter, an attempt is made to analyze Ezekiel's early poetry from critical point of view to form and confirm a view on Ezekiel's poetry. Chapter fifth of the book analyses the reflection of Indian ethos and culture in poetry written in his recent phase of life. And the last chapter of the book is the conclusion.

Works Cited

Abidi, S.Z.H. *Studies in Indo Anglian Poetry.* Bareilly: Prakash Book Depot, 1978., 287. Print.

Clemen, Carl. *Religions of the World.* New Delhi: Cosmo P, 2005. 94-108. Print.

Daruwalla, Keki N. (ed.). *Two Decades of Indian Poetry 1960-1980.* New Delhi: Vikas, 1980. 56. Print.

"Define Ethos & Explain Features of Indian Ethos." Web. 11 January 2016.

Devarajan, R. Indian Ethos in Management. *The Hindu Business Line.* December 6, 2005, 34. Print.

"Ethos." Wikipedia. Org. Web. 25 April 2016. (https://en.m.wikipedia.org)

Ezekiel, Nissim. *Collected Poems.* New Delhi: O.U.P., 2005, 12. Text.

Garman, Michael. "Nissim Ezekiel: Pilgrimage and Myth". *Journal of South Asian Literature* (Spring-Summer 1976): 212. Print.

Harrex, S.C. "Small Scale Reflection on Indian English Language Poetry." *The Journal of Indian Writing in English* (January-July 1980): 145. Print.

Iyengar, K.R.S. *Indian Writing in English*. New Delhi: Sterling, 1984, 649. Print.

Karnani, Chetan. *Nissim Ezekiel*. New Delhi, Arnold Heinemann 1974, 105-68. Print.

Khanna, Meeta. Critical Tenets of Nissim Ezekiel's Poetry: A Perspective. *International Journal of English Language, Literature and Humanities* (2015): 592. Print.

Khan, Eshanullah. *The Evolution of the Religious and Social Life of Man*. New Delhi: Bait-At-Hikmat Trust, 1989, 43. Print.

King, Bruce. *Modern Indian Poetry in English*. Delhi: OUP, 1987, 1. Print.

Lal, P. *Modern Indian Poetry in English*. Calcutta: Writers Workshop, 1969, 5. Print.

Molloy, Michael. *Experiencing the World's Religions: Tradition, Challenge, and Change*. California: Mayfield Publishing Company, 1999, 71-108. Print.

Murugan, Seema. *The Fiction of Alice Walker: A Study of Black Image*. Delhi: Authorspress, 2008, 5. Print.

Nehru, Jawaharlal. *The Discovery of India*. New Delhi: Jawaharlal Nehru Memorial Fund and O.U., 1958, 86-268. Print.

"New International Webster's Comprehensive Dictionary of the English Language." *Encyclopedic Edition*. Naples Florida: Trident Press International, 2004, 314-36. Print.

Pandey, Mithilesh K. *Contemporary Indian Literature in English, A Humanistic Perspective*. Kalyani P, New Delhi, 1999, 12. Print.

Parthasarathy, R. ed., *Ten Twentieth-Century Indian Poets*. OUP, 1976. 7. Print.

Shahane, Vasant A. "The Religious Philosophical Strain in Nissim Ezekiel's Poetry". *Journal of South Asian Literature*. (1976): 254. Print.

Wesly, John, and Chandra, N.D.R. Cultural Complexity in Nissim Ezekiel's Works. *The Criterion: An International Journal in English*. 3.3 (2012): 2. Web. 24 April 2016.

2 Nissim Ezekiel as an Indian Poet

Understanding Ezekiel's personal life, his surrounding, his poetic career, his failure and success is of great worth in making him an Indian poet. In fact, all these aspects help to reflect Indian ethos and culture in his poetry. The present chapter also attempts to study the influences of other poets on his poetic career. To discuss some of his prominent poems in order to study the impression of Indian ethos and culture is equally emphasized in this chapter. Lastly, the chapter makes a brief estimate of Ezekiel's craftsmanship and technique which contribute in making him a poet of a great rank.

It is observed that Ezekiel's biography is related to his poetry. In fact, his poetry is the outcome of his personal quest for identity and concern for the people. It does not matter that he was born a Jew, what touches is his surrounding and his acceptance of Indian environment. A person is not identified by his caste or religion, but by the place where he has grown up, lived and contributed in his field. Therefore, his childhood, his early education, his mother tongue, his experiences at school and college, his family background, his placement in various jobs, his experiences while earning money, his foreign visits, his participation in various programs, his youth, married life and so on are of sole significance in making him a poet.

As far as the study of Ezekiel's biography is concerned, he was grown up and lived in Indian environment. This environment shaped his poetic personality, gave him unique Indian identity and accepted him as an Indian poet. While discussing Indian ethos and culture in Ezekiel's poetry, it is necessary to keep in mind his intentions to be rooted in India. However, being rooted in the culture of land it is not difficult to call Ezekiel as a critic of Indian ethos and culture.

Nissim Ezekiel was born in a Chawl of the Byculla Bridge in Bombay on 16 December 1924 to Moses Ezekiel Talkar and Diana of Jewish (Ben-Israel) parents. His father was a lecturer in Biology at Wilson College and mother was a teacher in a school founded by her. Second among five brothers and sisters, Ezekiel was primarily admitted to the Convent of Jesus and Mary, a school run by Christian missionaries in Bombay. It was in school his interest in reading poetry was developed and his fascination of it began to awake the poet in him. Ezekiel's reading of a poem in classroom gave him a kind of excitement.

Thus, Ezekiel composed his first poem at the age of twelve. His teacher appreciated the poem. She referred to him as a poet. He recalls that moment in the words: "That moment determined my vocation for me. I've never really stopped after that, except for spells of genuine sterility" (qtd. in Kumar 165). One can develop interest in a thing when someone appreciates it. It can be a kind of motivation. The same happened in the life of Ezekiel and then he never stopped.

Later he studied in Antonio D'souza High school of "Background, Causally" and remained there until 1941 where Raj Kapoor, the Hindi film personality, was among his classmates. Raj Kapoor was possibly one of "... the strong/ But undernourished Hindu lads" (*CP* 179). Ezekiel read Bhagavad Gita in English translation while on vacations in 1939 at his grandfather's house in Tal, in rural Maharashtra. His most beautiful poem "Night of the Scorpion" may be based on the actual experiences he had during one of such visits to his village.

It was his school Fathers who criticized Hinduism which compelled Ezekiel to grow interest in the Hindu texts. In his interview, Ezekiel states:

> ... I was after all, in a Roman Catholic school, and the Fathers used to say to the students that there was nothing in Hinduism. The Hindus, Parsis, Muslims, all said, What? There is nothing in Hinduism? So we started reading Gita and the Upanishads at school which I may not have done in the next ten years had the Fathers not said there was nothing in it. (Ezekiel, "An Interview with Nissim Ezekiel" 163)

It shows clear cut impact of Gita and Upanishads and therefore of Hinduism on his writings. It helps him to reveal the Indian ethos and culture in his poetry. It also confirms his rootedness in Indian tradition and its religious practices.

After his early schooling, he joined the four-year B.A. course at Wilson College, Bombay and graduated in English Literature with a first class in 1945. He completed his post graduation in English from the University of Bombay. His name appeared in the list of successful students at the M.A. examination in 1947 and won the prestigious R.K. Lagu prize. Ezekiel, as an undergraduate, came under the influence of M.N. Roy in Wilson College, Bombay and became the active member of his Radical Democratic Party. His contact with M.N. Roy had a formative influence on Ezekiel's poetic career and this had helped him to widen the humanistic horizon of his personality:

> I've attempted to put into poetry as much as has happened to me. But actually what has gone into it is fairly limited, considering the time and energy spent on politics. I became a Royist at the age of 18. It went with rationalism, atheism, anti-religious convictions, the whole international movement which was partly Marxist-influenced. Indian society was to be made democratic, secular and scientific. That phase in my life lasted from 1942 to 1947, though I stopped being Royist in 1951. (De Souza 75)

His creativity did not allow him to keep quite. A few of his poems appeared in the magazine of the college where he studied. His college friend, Balu Patel, introduced him to modern poetry and to modern literature. He composed a number of poems in his college days. The first to appear in a general magazine was in K.M. Munshi's *Social Welfare*. It was the beginning of formation of a poet in Ezekiel's poetic career. He was appointed to teach English Literature at Khalsa College, Bombay. He taught at school, at college and at university. He was primarily a teacher both in life and poetry. As Gieve Patel puts:

> When he conducts programs on art appreciation for Bombay television, he teaches. When he sits in his industry office at the Indian P.E.N. as its most active office bearer, reading quantities of other people's poems and giving his comments on them—thereby earning lifelong friends and enemies—he is teaching again. When he writes his poetry he teaches, this time largely himself. In all these contexts the pedagogic bone is relieved, even subverted, by self-directed irony, subdued passion, and simple, direct concern for what's at hand. (17)

Thus, his experience as a teacher of English literature for a number of years at Bombay University shaped his literary personality.

However, his participation in Indian scene could not hold Ezekiel for long. A passion to see beyond the Indian horizon tempted him to visit England. Meanwhile, his friend Ebrahim Alkazi, a famous theatre personality, helped him and arranged a one-way steamer ticket. Ezekiel sailed off in *Jal Azad* and reached London in November 1948 after undertaking a twenty-six-day voyage at sea. He, initially, stayed with Alkazi and earned a clerical post in the Internal Affairs Department of the Indian High Commission at London to meet his expenses there. Actually, his job was to edit a weekly newsletter for the commission. He took much interest in the work. He registered for a B.A. in Philosophy at Birbeck College, affiliated to the University of London and studied under the legendary philosopher C.E.M. Joad. However, he could not complete the course due to insufficient time. Then he decided to resign the job at India House in order to take full time to writing and earning a pound here and there by sending poems and reviews to British journals like *Strand Magazine*. He moved from Alkazi's flat and found accommodation in the basement of the same building as referred in "Background, Casually"—"Philosophy / Poverty and Poetry, three / Companions shared my basement room" (*CP* 179).

Ezekiel's visit to England to study philosophy under C.E.M. Joad at Birkbeck College was unique. During his stay for three and a-half years in England, he not only concentrated on philosophy but also showed interest in the theatre, cinema and art to psychology and modern Indian culture. He met Keshav Malik, the first literary editor of *Thought*, a political journal started in 1948 in New Delhi, who was there to attend the inaugural function of the Congress for Cultural Freedom. C.R. Mandy, the editor of *The Illustrated Weekly of India*, requested him to send his poems for publication. In fact, his interest grew in composing poems in London.

It was in England Ezekiel's creative efforts bore fruits and he had his first book of poems, *A Time to Change,* published by *Fortune Press*, London in 1952. At that time, Ezekiel, in his early twenties, gradually discovered himself to be an authentic poet. The poet, therefore, decided to dedicate himself to this noble aim. "The poet in him grew and developed as much out of his intellectual mental make-up as out of an emotional make-up and one finds in his poetry a close and meaningful interaction between the philosopher and the poet" (Ramamurthi 123). In this way, he left England receiving a label as a poet and it was the beginning of his poetic career that shows poetry was the powerful passion of his life.

Ezekiel has performed several important roles in his life, which contributed in making him as a critic of Indian ethos and culture. He was the editor of *Quest, Imprint* and *The Illustrated Weekly of India*. He broadcast on art and literature for the Bombay station of the All India Radio. He was a visiting professor at the University of Leeds and at a number of American colleges and universities. He was also Director of a Theatre Unit in Bombay. He also showed interest for some time in advertising—a fact that gave him some insight into the advertising techniques of Indian-English poets (Karnani 7).

Ezekiel was married to Daisy Jacob at the Magen David Synagogue on 23 November 1952. This event shaped the material for his poem "Jewish Wedding in Bombay". Ezekiel's second book of verse *Sixty Poems* was published in 1953 by the *Strand Bookshop*, Bombay. While writing this collection, he was just warming up for his later work. Unfortunately, there was a fall in standards. This collection proved an anti-climax after the success of his first volume. *Sixty Poems* has given 'a sense of continuity' to his life and he decided to publish these poems. The next year, he took to advertising with Shilpi Advertising concern as a copywriter. He was appointed as the first editor of the *Quest* in 1955. In 1956, Ezekiel visited America and worked there for six months as the manager of Shilpi. He visited several American universities during his stay in America and sharpened the poetic talent in him.

After five years, Ezekiel published his third volume of poems named *The Third* in 1958. It showed remarkable maturity which helped him to use it in his next volume. He left the Shilpi in 1959 and joined as General Manager for picture-frame manufacturing company, Chemould, where he wrote all the poems of *The Unfinished Man.* The year 1959 proved poetically the most important in his life. In the same year, he wrote *The Unfinished Man* and was published in 1960. It is the only book of Ezekiel, which has run into a second edition, with introduction and notes by Eunice de Souza. It brought name and fame to the poet. It also earned the tribute from Adil Jussawala: "the most perfect book of poems written by Indian English...Ezekiel at his most honest and lyrical best" ("The Journal of Commonwealth Literature" 69). In 1961, he got associated with *Imprint* as an Associate Editor in charge of the reviews section for seven years. Then Ezekiel became more successful as a critic of repute with his perceptive and influential criticism on literature, and arts.

In June 1961, he became lecturer and head of the Department of English in Mithibai College of Arts, Vile Parle, Bombay and worked there for eleven years. R. Parthasarathy was there among his junior colleagues and this association seems to have been of great importance to the development of post-colonial poetry in India. His fourth volume *The Exact Name* was published by the *Writers Workshop* in 1965. He also started writing the Poetry India in 1966 and its six issues included modern poetry in various Indian languages.

Ezekiel visited America for the second time in March 1967 and stayed with A.K. Ramanujan at the University of Chicago. During this visit, Ezekiel held his sessions of poetry and delivered lectures in various universities on Indian Writing in English. The same year proved a significant milestone in his life for he took LSD trips for the first time which had an important impact on his poetry "a starting point for a self-transforming process". He rediscovered the divine aspect of life through his several LSD trips between 1967 and 1972.

Ezekiel's creativity could not spare him to develop love for theatre. It was his friendship with Ebrahim Alkazi which attracted him toward theatre. This intimacy, however, led him to the literary advantages as he himself put in an interview:

> I became interested in the theatre through my association with E. Alkazi and his work in Bombay's Theatre Group. Later, we formed the Theatre Unit. To write plays became at that time a dream for me and to some extent it is still a dream. More than 15 years passed after my first 5 plays were written, and I regret the lapse but expect to make up for it before the end of 80s. (Sharma 42)

In 1969, the *Writers Workshop,* Calcutta published his collection *Three Plays* ("Nalini," "Marriage poem" and "The Sleepwalkers") and the journal *Enact* brought out his "Song of Deprivation" in its July issue. *Encounter, The Illustrated Weekly of India, London Magazine* and *The Spectator* published his many other poems. He has frequently changed his jobs, but all the time he remained a dedicated Indian poet. He was reader in the department of English, Bombay University where, in collaboration with a Marathi Scholar, Vrinda Nabar, he translated into English the Marathi work, "Snake-Skin and Other Poems" of Indra Sant in 1974.

In 1974, Ezekiel went to America on a cultural Exchange Programme of the Government of the United States and gave readings from his works. His sixth poetic volume *Hymns in Darkness* brought out by *Oxford University Press* in 1976. Gradually Ezekiel had achieved an international fame as a contemporary poet. As a result of it, the American periodical, *Journal of South Asian Literature* (1976) published a special issue on him. The same year, Ezekiel attended the International Colloquium on the Inter-Cultural Encounters in Literature at the East-West Centre, Hawaii as a delegate. There he got a Professional Associate Award. Besides, he was honoured with the Excellence Award for his contribution to poetry on 30 April 1976. The publication of his journal *Quest* was stopped due to Emergency in the mid-seventies and he started editing *Freedom First*, a fortnightly based on literary and intellectual pursuits. He read poetry at Rotterdam International Poetry Festival from 11-17 June 1978 and during the same event *Latter-Day-Psalms*, the poem, was written.

Jane Swamy scripted and directed a film *Picture a Poet* which was premiered at the Alliance Francaise in Bombay in 1981. The film begins with a voice-over of "Background, Casually," the voice being Ezekiel's itself. Ezekiel's seventh volume of poems, *Latter-Day-Psalms* (1982) won for him the Sahitya Akademi cultural award in 1983. This volume has also been translated into Assamese. He attended the Edinburgh Arts Festival in 1983 and participated in poetry reading session. He responded the event by writing "Edinburgh Interlude-Lightly" which appeared in xeroxed form in the same year. He visited Germany and participated in literary discussions and reading. He also chaired the international panel of judges for Commonwealth International Poetry Award in 1986. His special issue Nissim Ezekiel was published by *Journal of Indian Writing in English* in the same year. He attended the conference 'India Forty Years after Independence' at Canada in 1987 and in the same year, he went to Hong Kong.

Ezekiel was honoured with the Padmashri Award by Government of India for criticism in 1988. He attended New Zealand International Festival of Arts in 1988 and was invited as guest lecturer at the Adelaid Book Fair, Australia and Wellington in the same year. He was invited at the National University of Singapore. His *Singapore Sequence,* unpublished poems are the parts of this South-Asian experience. His *Collected Poems* (1952-1988) was published by *Oxford University Press* in 1989.

Apart from a poet, Ezekiel could not stop writing prose and as a result, his prose writing appeared as *Selected Prose* in 1992. His sixteen days tour to England in February 1993 as a guest of the Arts Council of Great Britain was unique in respect of adding some poetic experiences to his personality. Meanwhile, he was hospitalized for the treatment of hernia. Despite casual sickness, Ezekiel continued his literary activities. Later, he visited the Banaras Hindu University to deliver the Professor Vikramaditya Rai Memorial Lecture on "The Infinite Aspects of Critical Writing" on 6-7 September 1994. During his stay at Banaras, he was introduced to the Buddhist pilgrim-centre at Sarnath. His last work, the play "Don't Call It Suicide" published in 1994. His last article "Poetry in the Time of Tempest" was appeared in *Sunday Times* on 29 June 1997.

Ezekiel's mental capacity was seen declined on many incidents in the past by his friends, admirers, students and the family members. He had collapsed at an American Jewish Joint Distribution Committee meeting in Bombay in August 1998 and had to be hospitalized at the Shushruta Nursing Home at Dadar. He suffered from Alzheimer's disease. Later on, he was shifted to the A.J. Dias Nursing Home at Bandra, Bombay where he struggled for life. He died in Mumbai on 9 January 2004. His death was an unbearable shock for the literary world. It was really painful for his admirers. Jerry Pinto expressed gratitude for Ezekiel in *Mid Day*: "Nissim Ezekiel died yesterday. He had just turned 80. I do not feel as if I have lost a friend, a colleague and a fellow worker in the salt mines of the world. The onset of Alzheimer's meant that we, Mumbai, its poets, his friends and I lost him by degrees" ("Pinto").

Bruce King also pays him a tribute in the words:

> By the time of his death Ezekiel's place and contribution to Indian literature and culture were clear. The obituaries, reminiscences, and homage spoke of him as a nationalist, recalled his decision to return to India, and that unlike many Indian Jews he had not moved to Israel, how he had forged a contemporary poetic language for Indian poetry in English, and his contribution to the intellectual life of the nation, especially in Bombay. A year after his death a national conference to discuss Ezekiel's role in Indian culture was held at Banaras University. (King, "Modern Indian Poetry in English" 8)

As a keen observer of life, Ezekiel never forgot to reflect Indian ethos, culture, attitude, art, and literature in his poetry. In his treatment of various themes such as love, sex, death, loneliness, treatment of women, superstitions, blind beliefs, he seems more a critic of Indian ethos and culture than he is a poet. These themes, however, try to express his personal quest for identity. There can be no writing that is 'nationally' unmarked, and Ezekiel himself has noted: "A writer needs a national or cultural identity, without that you become a series of imitations, echoes, responses, but you do not develop because there is nothing at the core to develop" (Beston 101). It reveals his attitude of commitment; the one basis to him is to his environment. He further says of himself: "I am not a Hindu and my background makes me a natural outsider!

Circumstances and decisions relate me to India. In other countries I am a foreigner. In India I am an Indian" (Ezekiel, "Naipaul's India and Mine" 88).

In fact, Ezekiel's poetry reveals his personal dilemma working in the direction of complexities of existence in the post-Independent India. "Ezekiel's poetry is the both instrument and the outcome of his attempt as a man to come to terms with himself. One finds in his poems the imprint of a keen, analytical mind trying to explore and communicate on a personal level, feelings of loss and deprivation" (Parthasarathy 28).

During his stay in England, he lived in the company of philosophy, poverty and poetry. Nevertheless, in India he enjoyed a comfortable Indian poetic career. One cannot avoid that India is a playground for him to prove his national identity. He solemnly declares that he is very much an Indian and that his root lies deep in India. Ezekiel makes it clear, "India is simply my environment. A man can do something for and in his environment by being fully what he is, by not withdrawing from it. I have not withdrawn from India" ("Naipaul's India and Mine" 88). His genuine commitment to India and Bombay is outstanding as explained in his poem "Background, Casually". Nissim Ezekiel is so typically unBritish or un-American or un-anything else that if he is closer to any national sensibility, it is to Indian sensibility. He has asserted: "I regard myself essentially as an Indian poet writing in English I have a strong sense of belonging, not only to India, but to this city" (qtd. in Abidi 291).

Despite his foreign origin, there is no question of alienation for Ezekiel. His being of Jewish descent in a Hindu culture denies the problem of Ezekiel's alienation. This is a distinguishing theme of his poetry, which perhaps proves his Indianness for his acceptance of the Indian ethos and culture with all its paradoxes. "The alienation that arises from Ezekiel's communal identity is only one of the alienation games life has forced him to play. As we saw, the poet attempts to overcome this alienation by a fantastic and contemptuous acceptance of the overwhelming Hindu environment" (Rao 102).

Ezekiel's involvement in Indian scenes is seen from three elements of his life and works which contribute in making him an Indian poet. These three elements include his conflict between the personal and the social, his contribution as a social critic, and his rootedness:

> I would like to underline three elements of Ezekiel's life and work that have shaped his career as a writer and have something to do with his involvement in public life. The first is traceable to his lifelong conflict between the personal and the social or what Bruce King describes as the conflict between 'desire and ethics'.... Secondly, Ezekiel felt need to speak out from time to time. This need to be a public commentator, reflected in his role as editor of books and periodicals, satisfied a deep urge in him to be true to his own self by being part of a larger community.... Thirdly, he identified with his community and that identity was an important source of his strength. This does not mean that he was communal in any sense. Far from it, he was the quintessential cosmopolitan democrat who recognized the importance of public institutions. (Ramkrishnan 461-62)

In a process of formation of a poet, the influence of other poet's work plays a necessary part. Because a genuine poet cannot compose a great poetry until he is impressed by other's works. Ezekiel is not exception to it. He is not only influenced by Indian-English poets, but also by certain dominant figures of his times. In case of Ezekiel, it proved bliss to gain his poetry a worldly fame. The influence of Rainer Maria Rilke is seen on his poetry. He learned from the influence of great German mythmaker that poetry required silence and solitude. In this respect, Chetan Karnani says: "His early prayer was for quietude. He wanted to seek the life of solitude and meditation. This ideal of Rilke is strongly expressed in these poems" (30).

On the other hand, mere imitation does not prove the metal of own's originality. Ezekiel followed the principles of the later and not the sole work as it is. He, himself, opposes the charges. Ezekiel says: "If someone were to say, 'Ah, but in these poems in an early book there are echoes of Rilke and Eliot,' I would agree. This does not mean that I produced a whole poem which is nothing but Rilke. If there were some poems like that, I don't think I published them" (qtd. in Mishra 14).

Ezekiel was influenced by Yeast's treatment of poetry as the method of discovering oneself at the various stages in one's life. In his statement the Irish poet has said of his poetry: "It is myself that I remake" and Ezekiel, in his "Foreword" to *Sixty Poems*, said that "There is in each (poem) a line or phrase, an idea or image, which helps me to maintain some sort of continuity in my life" (Karnani 27). It seems that the Yeatsian impact is obvious in *Sixty Poems*. In "The Stone," the image seems to have been appeared from Yeasts' "Easter 1916". The title of his fourth volume, *The Unfinished Man* is also taken from Yeasts' poem "A Dialogue of Self and Soul":

> The ignominy of boyhood; the distress
>
> Of boyhood changing into man;
>
> The unfinished man and his pain
>
> Brought face to face with his own clumsiness… (*CP* 115)

Perhaps, Ezekiel permitted his *Sixty Poems* to be published because they had 'personal importance'. It seems that Ezekiel follows Yeasts' philosophy that poets, like women, "must labour to be beautiful," and the poem "Poet, Lover, Birdwatcher" is a suitable example where the poet refers "The best poets wait for words" (*CP* 135) like a lover waiting for his beloved till she "no longer waits but surrendering".

T.S. Eliot's influence on the twentieth century poets has been so pervasive that no poet of the substance remains untouched by him. Ezekiel has not been exception to it. In his obituary on Eliot, Ezekiel says:

> Eliot's poetry from 1917 to 1943 is like the Himalayan Mountains, with the Everest of The Waste Land several all but inaccessible peaks, a score or so of attractive but treacherous ranges (A Song For Simeon, Marina, et al.) and a miscellany of small, steep hills obscured in mist. The Quartets from a spacious, high plateau among the clouds. The air is rarefied but gracing, the winds are strong and chilly. The temptation to remain in this mountain-space and to accept it as the only sovereign territory of poetry was irresistible to several generations of readers. ("Eliot's Language: Thirst and Fear" 8)

Ezra Pound equally influenced Ezekiel to some extent. Ezekiel accepted that the American Imagist motivated him both thematically and technically:

> The early influence on me of Pound and Eliot concerned poetry as an art, as well as on criticism of poetry, of society past and present, of modes of thinking and feeling, etc. But I never accepted the doctrines which Pound and Eliot, separately defined for themselves and their readers. I sorted them out for myself, modified them to suit my temperament, and so on. It would be misleading and unfair to say that Pound and Eliot influenced me only on the "technique side". Their influence was far-reaching, even comprehensive, but I was never dominated by it. I used it and went back to it from time to time, noting how my growth changed my attitudes to their outstanding creative as well as critical writing. (Sharma 44)

Movement poets like Philip Larkin and Donald Davie influenced Ezekiel's poetry in its subject matter, self irony and allegory. Larkin and his contemporaries insisted that poetry ceased to be an instrument of propaganda. Like Larkin, Ezekiel treated both separately, the romantic vagaries and the patriotic strain of pre-Independence poetry. In this manner, Chetan Karnani puts:

> I am agree with David McCutchion who has rightly commented that Ezekiel "belong with Thom Gunn, R.

> S. Thomas, Elizabeth Jennings, Anthony Thwaite, and others like them. He has their cautions, discriminating style, precise and analytical, with its conscious rejection of the heroic and the Passionate as also of the sentimental and cosy. (qtd. in Karnani 172)

On the other hand, though others have influenced Ezekiel, he applied his own creative mind that sought a unique fruit. "You do not find him struggling to write like Eliot or Pound. There are, inevitably, echoes from other poets but the voice is Ezekiel's, and unmistakably so" (Acharya 154).

Ezekiel has not only been influenced by others, but also influenced other Indian-English poets and made his position strong as an Indian poet. In fact, Ezekiel has been not only a good poet himself but also the cause of good poetry in others. Many Indian-English poets took important lessons from him. P. Lal learns craft from Ezekiel's corrections. As P. Lal says, "I do not think I shall forget the time Ezekiel as Editor of *Quest*..., returned a poem I had sent him for possible publication. He twitted me for using an exclamation mark, chided obvious poeticism and sentimental reiteration" (Ezekiel, "The Unfinished Man" 2). Dom Moraes considers him as his Guru in the art of verse: "When Ezekiel spoke to me of his views on poetry, it was as though he had unlocked a box full of unheard whispers" (Ezekiel, "My Son's Father" 87). In this way Ezekiel has been proved a guiding star to Indian-English poetry. In this respect Bruce King observes:

> Ezekiel however, remained a continuing influence on Indian poetry as poet, literary critic, editor, publisher, teacher, adviser and friends of poets. His first volume despite the small number of copies printed came to the notice of a generation of budding poets many of whom, like Kersey Katrak, would cite or reply to Ezekiel's work in their own poetry. It was modern, intellectual, showed the influence of such twentieth century (then still somewhat controversial) masters as W.B. Yeats, T.S. Eliot, W.H. Auden in its dramatization of the self,

> purity of image and concern with technique while sharing with the British Movement poets of the 1950's an anti-romanticism and rational clarity a commonsense view of life. ("Three Indian Poets" 20)

Ezekiel's achievement as an Indian poet is beyond the imagination of a common student of English literature. He liberated Indian English poetry from the excessive bondage of the British Romantic and Victorian poets who influenced the pre-Independence poets in choice of the themes and styles. As a modernist, Ezekiel even fought a triumphant battle with the established pre-independence poets to make Indian English poetry more Indian than English in nature, attitude and form. Even the syntax and intonation of English employed by Ezekiel reflect the Indian sperm of the language. Besides, he succeeds to evoke the very spirit from Indian milieu and ethos in his poetry. It is through this transformation in his poetry, Ezekiel puts lot of impression on the post-Independence poets. Thus, these poets followed the advancement that Ezekiel brought in his poetry. They learnt the objectives of poetic creativity, namely, thematic and stylistic liberation.

Indeed, Ezekiel's poetry differs in theme and style of pre-Independence poets. A brief glance at poems of H.L.V. Derozio shows that his poetry carries an impact of John Keats and P.B. Shelley. In "The Harp of India," Derozio cannot escape from the stigma of imitativeness:

> And many a wreath for them did Fame
> of flowers still blooming on the minstrel's entwine grave:
> Those hands are cold—but if thy notes divine
> May be by mortal wakened once again,
> Harp of my country, let me strike the strain! (Derozio 1)

The great pioneer Derozio imitated the manner of Byron is evident in the above lines. While Ezekiel in his poem "In India" offers a glaring contrast both in theme and style:

> The Roman Catholic Goan boys
> The whitewashed anglo-Indian boys

The musclebound Islamic boys
Were earnest in their prayers. (*CP* 132)

In short, Ezekiel credited to bring about a shift in theme and style of Indian English Poetry, which was rooted in the influence of the British poets. Perhaps, this dive of freedom from the impact of the British poets on the pre-Independence poetry helped post-Independence poets to hire more accuracy and realism in representation of the Indian ethos and milieu in their poetry. Ezekiel's poetry shows inevitable reflection of the reality of the place to which he belongs. This remarkable achievement gives his poetry a special status in the realm of post-Independence poetry. It is praiseworthy on his part that he continued to be a true Indian in the later phase of his life, as he describes a Bombay street while traveling in Scotland in the following lines:

There's only this:
a tarred road
under a mild sun
after rain,
glowing;
wet, green leaves
Patterned flat
on the pavement
around dog-shit;
one ragged slipper
near an open gutter,
three crows
pecking away at it. (*CP* 220)

On the other hand, his childhood attachment to the city has brought a new dimension to his poetry. In his poem "City Song" he makes some observations:

As I sway in the breeze
The city sway below

Suddenly I learn
What I always know:
I don't wish to go any higher,
I want to return
As soon as I can,
To be of this city,
To feel its hot breath
I have to belong. (*CP* 223)

Thus, Indian ethos follows the dictum *Vasudhaiva Kutumbakam:* to consider the whole world as one's own family.

Ezekiel, indeed, earnestly attempts to give Indian English poetry a proper shape and make it original, remarkable Indian in character. Thus, Ezekiel played an important and essential role of a liberator and leader in changing the conventional face of Indian English Poetry. No one can hesitate to call him an Indian poet.

Moreover, Ezekiel creates the authentic Indian flavour by using Indian English as used by the Indian lower middle classes and proves his identity as an Indian poet. Ezekiel creates a typical Indian atmosphere by describing the Indian society. The persona's quarrel at the soap about the defective soap being given by the shopkeeper is all Indian:

Now small crowd is collecting
And shopman is much bigger than me,
And I am not caring too much
For small defect in well-known brand soap
So I'm saying
Alright OK Alright OK
This time I will take
But not next time. (*CP* 269)

An argument takes place due to that 'defective version of soap' and the shopkeeper loses his temper:

Now he is shouting
You Are Calling Me Blind Or What?
Come outside and I will show you
Then I am shouting
What you will show me
Which I haven't got already?
It is a vulgar thing to say
but I am saying it. (*CP* 269)

Again the poem is a comment on the use of English by semi-literate Indians. He portrays his characters with perfection. The characters are unique. Though they are individuals, they are typical.

In the poem "Occasion," the poet gives the sufferings of average Indian middle class where a typist is 'without a face or figure':

The typist says goodnight,
A south-Indian middle-aged balding man
Without a face or figure.
His name: Ramnathan or Krishnaswamy. (*CP* 277)

Tired of everyday life, many Indians speak the language, "I tell you, we should have left / This country twenty years ago / Now it's too late. There's no future for us" (*CP* 277).

Ezekiel also creates the South Indian atmosphere in his poetry:

At nowhere
or at Vanjipaiyalam
which is the same,
only the son is confident
and the crows.
The squawking of the crows here
is not just another distraction

but has its own integrity,
a clean, simple sound.
You recognise it
in its own right,
it belong so completely
with those shifting eyes,
sudden, flapping wings. ("Letter from the South")

Ezekiel's growing awareness of India is expressed in "And I reject the Indian Noise". No doubt, Indian environment is full of all sorts of noises. No Indian can deny and make indifference to these noises. These noises appear troublesome to those who have been staying abroad since long time. This happens with the poet as he expresses in the lines:

I shut it out
with symphonies
not meant to be heard
or news in languages unknown.
It is a form of self-defence:
one noise cancels out the other,
and I am free
underground or in the sky. (qtd. in Nandy 57)

But in the next part of the same poem, the poet tries to make it clear that these noises are important to put up with the Indian environment:

On rare occasions,
ragged spirit roused to scorn,
I play the ogre, striding out
to crush the vulgar source....
This does the job at last-
but only in my imagination. (qtd. in Nandy 57)

The poet becomes angry at the noisemakers when his mood is not tolerable. It happens on rare occasions. The poet imagines to stopping the noise but does not take action. This means that a true Indian cannot reject the environment at any cost:

> When the poet's mind feels contempt for the noise-makers, it forgets its compassionate quality. Then the poet becomes like a monster and rushes out of the house to shout at the people who are making the noise. But this is only enacting a fantasy. He doesn't actually succeed in action because he is unable to do anything against the noise. (Karnani 163)

The research earnestly attempts to focus all the concerning issues, which give an account of Indian ethos and culture in Ezekiel's poetry. In comparison to man in ancient India, modern man has grown so corrupt that he does not try to measure his hypocritical attitude in the limits of Indian culture. The poet points out, "Crocodile tears / Are unknown to crocodiles" (*CP* 209). Man has become a doll in the hands of illusion and has forgotten spirituality and morality. In his poem "Distance," the poet says, "I see myself enhanced and also small" (*CP* 192). Man's superficial growth loses his faith in god and makes him subject to ridicule himself, "I mock myself here / as if my very existence / is presumption". Man reaches to this condition because he makes "attempt to dance / without learning to walk". He thinks that secret of success is not hard work but hypocrisy, "The flattery and the bold advances / Were necessary after all / The minimum politics of survival and success" (*CP* 183).

On the other end, Indian saints and people are responsible for the degradation of moral and spiritual values because of their selfish attitude to God. The poet exposed the attitude of modern man in "The Second Candle":

> The second candle is for a miracle. I need
> A special favour, a certain turn of events
> What work alone will never bring,
> A gift we do not quite deserve
> But still may get by asking for it. (*CP* 296)

In modern age, other major poets have tried to prove their identity by one way or other. Nissim Ezekiel represents India by describing the Indian ethos and culture through English Language:

> In our time, each major English-speaking country can claim a poet who has made his region memorable through the use of that common foreign tongue—the English language. America with her Robert Lowell, Canada with Irving Layton, Australia with A.D. Hope, Ireland with Austin Clarke and Scotland with Hugh Macdiarmid. Ezekiel, in his own modest way, has tried to express the Indian ethos through the English language. His aspiration has been to give expression to the genius of the soul of India. Hence, he has never shown any desire to go and settle abroad. He is a poet of the city, Bombay, and remains rooted in that metropolitan soil. Except for a few short spells abroad, he has always remained in India. (Karnani 173)

In spite of the problem of English as a foreign language, many Indian poets played an important role in writing Indian poetry in English. Their contribution remains significant in seeking their national identity in one way or another. Nissim Ezekiel is one of them who attempts to reveal Indian attitude in his poetry and makes his identity as an Indian poet.

Ezekiel is an academic poet in more than one sense like Ramanujan and Parthasarathy. He was professor of English in Bombay University. Besides, his genius lays in poetry than he is an intellectual and a philosopher. Though he is rooted in a non-Indian, Jewish Parsi religion and culture, he is an Indian in his sensibility, beliefs and world-view. Thus, he occupies the foremost position among the modern Indian poets writing in English.

However, Ezekiel's technique, his use of imagery, irony, humour, meter, language etc. make him to stand in the line of other Indian poets writing in English. What strikes to readers in Ezekiel's poetry is his employment of apt and sharp imagery.

Though Ezekiel is not an imagist in any sense, his imagery wins the hearts of his readers. He creates an atmosphere of affection in his poetry with real, modern and simple images. He does not employ these images for mere decoration. However, they reflect his keen observation of Indian ethos and culture. The woman, the city and nature are the basic images used in his poetry. While other number of associate images recur round these three key-images and they acquire symbolic overtones for their frequent repetition.

The image of the pagan woman seems his favorite one for it appears repeatedly and as a great beast of sex, she is symbolic of seduction, mean passion, exploitation, corruption and defilement. As well, Ezekiel attacks the various organs of female body; the breast and thighs, flesh and hair, belly and torso, bone and marrow, lung and liver and eyes. In his poem "Motives," Ezekiel employs the images of various parts of female body:

It's easy to remember
your body in its nakedness.
I dwell on it as on a landscape
or a beloved painting
Not the total form only
but the details interest me
My motives are sexual,
aesthetic and friendly
in that order, adding up
to bed with you. (*CP* 154)

Ezekiel equally shows woman's requirement in "Encounter":

And after, sporting brown and green,
With her in white,
I knew that love is always right;
The might - have - been
Is worse than errors of the creed,

For in denying, still desires the deed. (*CP* 100)

Ezekiel, in his poem "Description," concentrates on a single image of hair:

I will begin-but how should I begin?
With hair, your hair,
remembered hair,
touched, smelt, lying silent there
upon your head, beneath your arms
and then between your thighs a wonder
of hair, secret
in light and in darkness
bare, suffering with joy
kisses light as air. (*CP* 48)

The beautiful image of hair is woven with other associate images of female body like 'head', 'arms' and 'thighs'. The different and even opposite images of woman occur in his other poems. If at one end the woman is pictured as the symbol of seduction, at the other, she is symbol of vitality, virtue and innocence. Perhaps Ezekiel aims to picture aesthetic aspect through the image of the woman. But it remains faint and shadowy. It finds connection between the image of pagan woman and the image of city in Nissim Ezekiel's poetry. Both the images represent defilement as well as degeneration of human heart. Ezekiel's commitment to 'self' and the city of Bombay inspires him to create images like the woman and the city.

Ezekiel's treatment of image of the basement room in "Background, Casually" brings out his inner self and his sickness for the 'home', a place where 'grace' is to be found. In "Poet, Lover, Birdwatcher," the poet very intellectually speaks of the usual 'patience' that lovers and ornithologist possess, like them, the poet waits for the spontaneous overflow of the words. Ezekiel employs the image of creation in his poem:

Subsided by dreams alone
The stubborn workman breaks the stone, loosens,

Soil, allows the seed to die in it, waits
Patiently for grapes or figs and even
Finds on a lucky day, a metaphor
Leaping from the soil. (*CP* 5)

Though Ezekiel is not a symbolist poet, he tries to apply intellectually perfect symbols through the medium of vivid imagery. As W. B. Yeats, a great symbolist poet handled the image of stone as the symbol of something, which is constant. Ezekiel says, "The stone is in the midst of all" (*CP* 204). Ezekiel uses a similar image in the lines:

I have learnt to revel in the stone,
Hard, cold, heavy, shapeless, solid stone,
To turn away from all that seems to flow
Elusively, time, water, blood around the bone. (*CP* 40)

Here the poet attempts to imitate the image of stone from Yeats, but lacks Yeats' grandeur and profundity. In this manner Chetan Karnani rightly remarks, "Such verse is not only loose in structure but diffuse in imagery". (Karnani 29). On the other hand, Ezekiel has the potential to create his own symbolic imagery as he himself puts it, "city, woman and nature certainly lend themselves to symbolic imagery". It means that symbolic imagery naturally comes to him.

Besides, his treatment of irony leads him to make his poetry a bit of social satire. In the following lines, one witnesses a witty and humorous exchange between a politician and his wife:

When the politician boasted
How he had made two hundred speeches,
'No, Tom,' his wife declared,
'You made the same speech two hundred times.' (*CP* 89)

Another amazing quality of Ezekiel's poetry is his versification. A close study of his poetry shows a gradual growth of his skill as a metrical artist. Despite his use of traditional meters and stanza form in the beginning, Ezekiel's metrical ability cannot be rejected. Even in his first collection *A Time to Change*, as Chetan Karnani points out "He not only made many experiments with prose rhythms but also showed a fine sense of structure and metrical ability" (Karnani 25). His poems like "Communication" and "History" reveal his mastery of the singing line. This singing quality is also seen in another collection *The Third*. Ezekiel is a lyric poet. In his poem "Declaration," he tries his best to capture rhythmical accuracy and a fine combination of sound and sense:

> Whatever is beyond my reach,
> I shall not reach, certain vases
> and women are too expensive, or else
> Fragile, exacting, best enjoyed
> from a distance, with delicate affection.
> Passion possesses, and beyond possession
> all is in question, mood and mystery spent,
> But reconciled to long perspectives
> The sensual form may serve to calm
> The senses and keep the darkness pure.
> Darkness, disturbed and turbulent,
> Is also dear: possession is necessary.
> Certain vases and women, however expensive,
> Fill the animal heart with wonder and warmth,
> And deprivation is desolation.
> I have stood in the empty room
> And gazed at crowds in the street,
> Longing to be absorbed
> No moral law can fill void,
> Deaf and blind to all is appetite. (*CP* 94)

This musical quality becomes more effective in *The Unfinished Man* with the power of imagination. In this connection S.T. Coleridge remarks: "The sense of musical delight and the power of producing it is the gift of imagination" (Cf.

Biographia Literaria). All the poems in this collection fascinate the readers for their rhythmical accuracy. He himself admits it at one place: "In rhythm I am at the flowing, the direct, the informal or conversational."

Ezekiel, in his recent poetry, has dropped the traditional verse-forms and the singing line and emphasized more on free verse. He also composed some prose poems. In his treatment of free verse, Ezekiel genuinely tried to achieve different effects. His use of free verse is suitable for the different moods and difficult thoughts. In his collection *The Exact Name,* his treatment of free verse is bewitching. His poem "Night of the Scorpion" shows this effect. In the words of Paul Verghese:

> Ezekiel's use of free verse is not an escape from the restraints imposed by a fixed form. He is well versed in the handling of metrical verse. In his free verse we find a rhythm that suits the emotional mood of the poem; the poet seeks a stricter discipline and arrives at what according to Marjore Boulton is the third kind of free verse—verse with a more colloquial style, suitable for the expression of difficult thought or sometimes of cynicism, of the man-of-world attitude. (qtd. in Tilak 45)

While analyzing Ezekiel's poetry, his use of language and diction is equally important. Ezekiel prefers simplicity, lucidity and clarity in the language. "Ezekiel loves simplicity in poetry as the most important virtue. Hence he chooses to speak from the heart to the heart" (Karnani 169). He rightly thinks that language and diction are important in order to attract the minds of readers. Therefore, in his poem 'Poet, Lover and Birdwatcher', he rightly says, "the best poets wait for words". Such painstaking craftsmanship can easily win the minds of the readers. His communicative efficiency is amazing. His use of easy language shows his hold on the minds of the readers. He avoids the heavy bombastic words and imparts a new and significance to colloquial and every day words. Even complicated and emotional themes are poetized in direct and simple words which is obvious in the lines from *Latter Day Psalms*:

How long are we to rely
On those marvelous things
in ancient Egypt? Tell me of the
marvelous things in Nazi Germany
Even with manna in our mouths,
We are not estranged from our lust. (*CP* 257)

Though Ezekiel seems economical in the use of language, he never seems obscure because of his simplicity, lucidity and clarity in the language as it is seen in the lines:

God grant me privacy...
God grant me certainty
In kinship with the sky,
Air, earth, fire, sea—
And the fresh inward eye. (*CP* 122)

Ezekiel artistically turns simple word into metaphor, images and symbols. In the following lines, the poet depicts human life with the help of similes and metaphors:

Rare is the man whose fruit is
in his season. Yet, his leaf
must wither, and that which
appears to prosper, is often
dying at the root. (*CP* 253)

Though Ezekiel is not an innovator with language, he uses vernacular words in his recent poetry. He further stressed the right of the poet to reform and recreate language. This is best seen in his poem "Goodbye Party for Miss Pushpa T.S." when he uses 'Pidgin' or 'Babu English'.

Ezekiel's outstanding command over language is quite noticeable. His diction is refined and polished, simple but pregnant with deep meaning, and evocative. His poetic style is marked with coolness. But at the same time lapidary quality adds a kind of clarity to the beauty of his poetic style. In fact, all these impart simplicity, lucidity, and clarity to his language. His language represents the national identity with keen observation of Indian aspirations, culture and attitude. "Ezekiel's mild, unemphatic delivery, a matter of cool diction, moderate metaphor, of syntax rather than music, fit his chosen stance as vigilant observer" (Naik 111).

It seems that Ezekiel's poetic craftsmanship is flawless. In this context, David McCutchion writes:

> Mr. Ezekiel achieves a laconic precision in which every word drops casually into place, yet fits perfectly into a strict scheme of rhyme and meter. The virtuosity and technical brilliance strongly suggest Auden...we find the same deft precision, the same mastery of a colloquial idiom, the personifications and generalized efforts, the stock phrases in new contexts, the juxtaposition of the commonplace and the erudite, the same compactness, startling appropriateness. (qtd. in Tilak 44)

Ezekiel achieves remarkable growth and development in technique. Artistic correlation between the thematic content and technique distinguishes his poetry. As William Walsh rightly comments:

> Ezekiel's poetry is lucid, rhythmically subtle, and scrupulously honest in its effort to be accurate, calm, and deliberate. At the same time, it is relatively less marked by resonance, imaginative vehemence or any richly metaphorical suggestiveness. Above all, it is clear, not in the sense of being simply explicable or paraphrasable, but seeming to move in an open, level, uncomplicated light. Part of this effect must be the consequence of a lack of constant connection with the living language in a society in which it is both the means and the measure of profound experience. The poetry gives the impression of steering to operate in a world in which the doors to the subconscious are, if not wholly almost shut. If poetry, as Coleridge said, is 'rationalized dream', then the emphasis in Ezekiel's poetry is very much on its rationality. (qtd. in Kumar 188)

Indeed, Ezekiel's poetic craftsmanship is completely modern with the quality of his skill, art, lucidity, clarity of expression, cool and evocative diction, suggestiveness, impressive imagery, biting irony, wit and humour, moderate metaphor, and absence of obscurity. "Ezekiel is perhaps the first Indian poet consistently to show Indian readers that craftsmanship is as important to a poem as its subject matter" (Jussawalla, "The New Poetry" 80).

In fact, the critical analysis of Ezekiel's poetry provides a platform in which the reflection of Indian ethos and culture has become a major part of his poetry. In reflecting Indian attitude, his personal quest for identity and concern for people play a vital role in his poetry. His contrast of tradition and modernity, his major themes of sex, love with reference to man-woman relationship, his technique, his employment of imagery, humour, irony as a weapon of satire, his use of free verse and traditional meters, and his use of lucid, clear, simple, colloquial language have helped to focus Indian ethos and culture to some extent.

A brief survey of Ezekiel's biography leads one to think that the seed of a poet has been sown in him from his childhood. He composed a poem at the age of twelve and that was the beginning of his poetic career. He came under the influence of many great poets. He visited England and returned India within three years with lot of poetic experience. He gathered lot of experience regarding the composition of poetry from various jobs. His most important occupation of a professor of English at Bombay University contributed to make him a poet.

In short, Ezekiel's poetry has reflected his personal anguish to settle down in India. It was the reason why he selected Indian scene in his poetry. As there is the reflection of his closeness to India and its environment, no one can reject Ezekiel's identity as an Indian poet. This is the emergence of Nissim Ezekiel as an Indian poet.

The above discussion, however, states his versatility, greatness and gifted poetic talent. What counts most in his poetry is the discovery of his Indianness. "Indianness is nothing but depiction of Indian culture" (Verghese 22). The factors shaping Ezekiel's talent as a poet, his biographical details, his likes and dislikes, his bent of mind etc. provided a fine platform to analyse Ezekiel as an Indian poet, which surely helps to locate Indian ethos and culture in his poetry. ".... he [Ezekiel] has availed himself of the composite culture of India to which he belongs, he must be said to be an important poet not merely in the Indian context but in a consideration of those that are writing poetry anywhere in English" (Narasimhaiah 40). In fact, it will not be wrong to call him as a critic of Indian ethos and culture.

In this chapter, an effort has been made to study Ezekiel's biography in order to see in what way Indian ethos and culture is reflected in his poetry. Indeed, craftsmanship is equally as important to a poem as its subject matter in terms of collecting the scattered petals of cultural ethos from his poetry. Therefore, a brief survey of his life, work and its major themes, his technique, his use of imagery, irony, humour, meter, language etc. is essential for making an estimate of Ezekiel as an Indian poet and to draw certain ideas to prove the hypothesis. Hence, the need of this chapter is proved.

Works Cited

Abidi, S.Z.H. *Studies in Indo Anglian Poetry.* Bareilly: Prakash Book Depot, 1978, 291. Print.

Acharya, N. Prabhakar. "Achievement and Failure in Nissim Ezekiel's Poetry." *Perspectives on Nissim Ezekiel.* Ed. S.C. Dwivedi. New Delhi: Kitab Mahal, 1989, 154. Print.

Beston, John B. "An Interview with Nissim Ezekiel", *Indian Writing in English,* ed. K.N. Sinha, New Delhi: Heritage, 1979, 101. Print.

Cf. *Biographia Literaria.*

Derozio, H.L.V. *Poems.* Calcutta: OUP, 1980, 1. Print.

De Souza, Eunice. "Interview with Four Indian English Poets", *The Bombay Review* 1, 1989: 75. Print.

Ezekiel, Nissim. *Collected Poems*. New Delhi: O.U.P., 2005. Text. All subsequent references to Ezekiel's poems shall be from this edition.

______. "Eliot's Language: Thirst and Fear," *Times of India*, 6 April 1989: 8. Print.

______. "An Interview with Nissim Ezekiel", *Selected Prose*. Delhi: Oxford, 1992. 163, Print.

______. "Lettter from the South." yet unpublished.

______. "My Son's Father." 87. Text.

______. "Naipaul's India and Mine." *New Writing in India*. ed. Adil Jussawalla, Harmondsworth, 1974. 88. Print.

______. "The Unfinished Man." 2. Text.

Jussawalla, Adil. *The Journal of Commonwealth Literature* 5 (July 1968): 69. Print.

______. 'The New Poetry.' *Reading in Commonwealth Literature*. Ed. William Walsh. Oxford: Clarendon Press, 1973, 80. Print.

Karnani, Chetan. *Nissim Ezekiel*. New Delhi: Arnold Heinemann 1974, 7-173. Print.

King, Bruce. *Modern Indian Poetry in English*. Delhi: OUP, 1987, 8. Print.

______. *Three Indian Poets*. Madras: Oxford, 1991, 20. Print.

Kumar, Satish. *A Survey of Indian English Poetry*. Bareilly: Prakash Book Depot, 2001, 165-88. Print.

Lall, Emmanuel Narendra. *The Poetry of Encounter*. New Delhi: Sterling P., 1983, 66. Print.

Mishra, Sanjit. *The Poetic Art of Nissim Ezekiel*. New Delhi: Atlantic Publishers and Distributors, 2001, 14. Print.

Naik, M.K. *Aspects of Indian Writing in English*. Macmillan, 2004, 111. Print.

Nandy, Pritish, Ed. *Indian Poetry in English Today*. New Delhi: Sterling Paperbacks, 1973, 57. Print.

Narasimhaiah, C.D. *The Swan and the Eagle*. Shimla: Indian Institute of Advanced Study, 1969, 40. Print.

Parthasarathy, R. *Ten Twentieth Century Indian Poets.* New Delhi: O.U.P., 1976, 28. Print.

Patel, Gieve. "Introduction" *Nissim Ezekiel: Collected Poems,* O.U.P., 1989, 17. Print.

Pinto, Jerry. *Mid Day Multimedia.* 10 January 2004: n. pag. Web. 15 Feb. 2016.

Ramamurthi, K.S. *Twenty-Five Indian Poets in English.* New Delhi: Macmillan, 123. Print.

Ramkrishnan, E.V. "My Background Place is Where I am: The Public Voice in Nissim Ezekiel's Poetry". *Nissim Ezekiel Remembered.* ed. Havovi Anklesaria. New Delhi: Sahitya Akademi, 2008. 461-62. Print.

Rao, K. Raghavendra. "The Alienation Games: The Poetry of Nissim Ezekiel". *Perspectives On Indian Poetry in English.* ed. M.K. Naik. New Delhi: Abhinav, 1984, 102. Print.

Sharma, Sushil Kumar. "Fourteen Questions to Nissim Ezekiel." *Essays on Nissim Ezekiel.* ed. T.R. Sharma. Meerut: Shalabh P., 1994, 42-44. Print.

Tilak, Raghukul. *New Indian English Poets and Poetry.* New Delhi: Rama Brothers, 1995, 44-45. Print.

Verghese, C. Paul. *Problems of the Indian Creative Writer in English.* Bombay: Somaiya P., 1971, 22. Print.

3 Indian Ethos and Culture in Indian English Poetry

This chapter attempts to highlight the reflection of Indian ethos and culture in the poetry of prominent contemporary Indian English poets in order to see if Nissim Ezekiel excels in the motive. It deals with the works of Ezekiel's contemporary prominent Indian English poets like A.K. Ramanujan, Kamala Das, R. Parthasarathy, Jayant Mahapatra, K.N. Daruwalla, Dom Moraes, Arun Kolatkar, Shiv K. Kumar, P. Lal, Gieve Patel, Pritish Nandy, Gauri Deshpande and many others.

The poets of post-Independence era bring the new spirit in modern Indian English Poetry and equally attempt to make it completely Indian. As Rajyalaxmi says:

> Our models have been neither exclusively Indian nor British, but "cosmopolitan". Europe, Africa, America and Asia have all become a part of our culture consciousness, offering impetus and stimulation. Our poets have been suddenly lifted from an exclusive to an extensive range of creative experience. They have been raised from a conservative to a cosmopolitan culture, to confront the new shape of things and acquire a new view of human destiny. The age has changed and requires a new image. This has been largely met by the poet. (qtd. in Rana 1)

The new poetry depicts new trends, but could not escape from the impact of tradition of the early poetry. The past shapes the future in the new poetry. It shows great impact of racial tradition, burning issues in the environment, blind beliefs, superstitions and Indian rivers, Vedas, Upanishads, Ramayana, and Mahabharata etc. Thus it reflects Indian ethos and culture to some extent. The exponents of the new poetry are rooted in India and they have shown their skills in depicting Indian society and culture with new insight and great favour. A.K. Ramanujan is only exception to it. But even being settled outside, Ramanujan's poetry explores his root in India.

A.K. Ramanujan is one of the Indian English poets in the post-Independence era. He is bi-lingual, for he writes both in Kannada and in English. Being settled outside, and cut off from his native environment, he still senses India's past, history and tradition. He suffers from homesickness in his poetry which experiences a nostalgic note and consequently finds his roots in Indian society. His poetry is "rooted in and stems from Indian environment and reflects its more, often ironically" (Parthasarathy 3). Through nostalgic vein, his poetry reflects Indian ethos and culture to some extent. His poetry "reflects a touch of humanity, Indian ethos and pertinence of life" (Gupta 1).

Ramanujan, a versatile writer, contributes two slender volumes—*The Striders,* and *Relations: Poems.* Besides, his translations include "Fifteen Tamil Poems" and "The Interior Landscape" is outstanding for they owe him Gold Medal of Tamil Writer's Association. The present work proposes to study prominent poems of Ramanujan.

Ramanujan in his poem "Snake" highlights the Hindu customs and rituals—that of offering milk to *nagas.* The poem exclusively exposes Hindu attitude of Indian mother to perform all rituals:

> Mother gives them milk
> in saucers. She watches them suck
> and bare the black-line design
> etched on the brass of the saucer.
> The snake man wreathes their writhing
> round his neck

for father's smiling
money. But I scream.
Sister ties her braids
with a knot of tassels. (Ramanujan 4)

The poem perfectly shows his attachment to the rituals performed in Hinduism. Even he could remember the rituals from his childhood recollection:

Now
frog can hop upon this sausage rope,
flies in the sun will mob the look in his eyes,
and I can walk through the woods. (Ramanujan 4)

Ramanujan's poetry is marked with references to father, mother, grandmother, sister, wife, cousin and so on. His attachment to his family becomes the concern of his poetry. On the other hand, he is preoccupied with inner and physical violence. The nostalgic strain is obvious in his "On the Very Possible Jaundice of My Unborn Daughter":

And if that daffodil too flaps all morning
in grandma's hands, how can my daughter
help those singing yellows
in the whites of her eyes? (Ramanujan 14)

Ramanujan's Indian memories of past are collected photographically with their fine and vivid pictures in his mind. As he remembers in poem "Still Another for Mother":

Something opened
in the past, and I heard something shut
like the heavy door
of my mother's black-pillared
nineteenth century
Silent house, given on her marriage day
to my father, for a dowry. (Ramanujan 15)

The line clearly depicts mother as the head of the family. The dowry system of India is also a legacy of Indian culture.

Ramanujan in his poem "A River," describes the historical river *Vaigai* in Madurai. The poet dives deep in Indian Culture and tradition. He also focuses other poets who sing the flood or the dryness in the river:

> The poets sang only of the floods.
> He was there for a day
> when they had the floods.
> People everywhere talked
> of the inches rising,
> of the precise number of
> cobbed steps
> run over by the water, rising
> on the bathing places. (Ramanujan 38)

Again, Ramanujan narrates:

> The new poets still quoted
> the old poets, but no one spoke
> in verse
> of the pregnant woman
> drowned, with perhaps twins in her,
> kicking at blank walls
> even before birth. (Ramanujan 38)

In short, he criticizes the old poets for not being in realistic temperament to reveal human concerns. He also raises finger at new poets who merely quote the old poets.

Ramanujan's another poem "Of Mothers, among Other Things" deals with the glory of mother. He has deep love for mother and describes her as a source of all happiness and pleasures. The mother is described as an image of patience and sacrifice in the poem:

> My cold parchment tongue licks bark

in the mouth when I see her four
still sensible fingers slowly flex
to pick a grain of rice from the kitchen floor. (Ramanujan 61)

"Love Poem for a Wife I" is one of the beautiful love poems in which Ramanujan presents his ambiguous situation to show his connectedness and disliking. The poet also reveals his difficulties imposed by the traditional attitude of society:

Really what keeps us apart
at the end of years is unshared
childhood. You cannot, for
instance,
meet my father. He is some
years
dead, neither can I meet yours:
he has lately lost his temper
and mellowed. (Ramanujan 65)

The poem "Small Scale Reflections on a Great House" focuses on the tradition of joint family in India. The daughter, son-in-laws, grandsons and so on live together in a great house to make it a universe. The house appreciates both, idiots and responsible:

Nothing stays out: daughter's
get married to short-lived idiots;
sons who run away come back
in grandchildren who recite Sanskrit
to approving old men, or bring
betelnuts for visiting uncles
who keep them gaping with
anecdotes of unseen fathers, (Ramanujan 98)

In "Obituary," Ramanujan on his father's death records the situation ironically. He speaks on Indian ceremonies and rituals especially related to the death. He describes the ritual:

Being the burning type,
he burned properly
at the cremation
as before, easily
and at both ends,
in the ashes that didn't
look one bit different,
several spinal discs, rough,
some burned to coal, for sons.
To pick gingerly
And throw as the priest
Said, facing east
Where three rivers met
Near the railway station;
No long-standing headstone
With his full name and two dates. (Ramanujan 111)

Indeed, Ramanujan is aware of his root in native land. Like Nissim Ezekiel, Ramanujan in his poetry could not escape from his past memories of Indian culture and tradition:

> Like Nissim Ezekiel, A.K. Ramanujan has a close look on each and every detail of the Indian life. His appreciation of Indian way of life does not depict his sense of appreciating own culture, but it provides a unique background to his poetic world. His sketches are not gloomy or full of pleasure, but tell the story of human existence with an ironic detachment. (Singh 162)

In his final estimate it appears that Ramanujan tries to pay homage to Indian ethos and culture. On the other hand, living in the soil, Ezekiel has given a perfect judgment to the reflection of Indian ethos and culture in his poetry.

Kamala Das alias Madhavikutty was born at Punnayurkulam in Malabar, Kerala in 1934. She destined to be a poet for she was born among such family members who were totally devoted to art and literature. Das was educated mainly at home. She is a bilingual for she writes both in Malayalam and English. She won PEN's Asian Poetry Prize for her remarkable poems. In 1984, she won Sahitya Akademi Award for her *Collected Poems*. Her renowned verse collections are *Summer in Calcutta* (1965), *The Descendants* (1967), *The Old Playhouse and other Poems* (1973) and *Collected Poems*. Her autobiography *My Story* published in 1975. She writes poetry with a feminine touch. She is known for her directness, frankness and candidness in order to hit age-old tradition and convictions in her poetry. She is a confessional poet. Her poetry is marked with various themes such as love and sex, body, decay and death, city life and so on.

Das is basically a poet for the cause of woman. She voices against the male-dominated world where women are treated badly. In her poem "Afterwards," she expresses her hope and fear for womankind:

> Son of my womb,
> Ugly in loneliness.
> You walk the world's bleary eye
> Like a girt. Your cleverness
> Shall not be your doom
> As ours was. (K. Das, "Summer in Calcutta" 55)

The line exclusively expresses a mother's attachment to her son. In her own life Das could not realize the ecstasy of love. Perhaps, she is disappointed in her married life for she exposes the hollowness and tiresomeness of a married life:

> I shall someday leave, leave the cocoon
> You built around me with morning tea,
> Love-word flung from doorways and of course
> Your tired lust. I shall someday take
> Wings, fly around, as often petals
> Do, when free in air, and you dear one
> Just the sad remnant of a root, must

> Lie behind, sans pride, on double beds
> And grieve. (K. Das, "Summer in Calcutta" 52)

Das longs to fly in the air freely without any restrictions. In fact, she seems to be struggling to find the self beyond the physical. Such sensitive poetry of Kamala receives a better appreciation from fairer sex. It happens that Das is not happy in her married life. Therefore, she tries to express her suppressed desires of unfulfilled love. Kamala Das says, "My husband was immersed in his office-work, and after work there was the dinner, followed by sex. Where was there any time left for him to want to see the sea or the dark buffaloes of the slopes?" (K. Das, "I have Lived Beautifully" 41). In her poem "A Relationship," she exposes her loneliness:

> Yes,
> It was my desire that made him male
> And beautiful, so that when at last we met
> To believe that once I knew not his
> From, his quiet touch, or the blind kindness
> Of his lips was hard indeed. Betray me?
> Yes, he can, but never physically. (qtd. in Dwivedi 23)

"The Freaks" attempts to focus Mrs. Das' predicament as a married woman. She highlights her misery:

> Nothing more alive than the
> Skin's lazy hungers? Who can
> Help us who have lived so long
> And have failed in love? The heart,
> An empty cistern, waiting
> Through long hours, fills itself
> With coiling snakes of silence.
> I am a freak. It's only
> To save my face, I flaunt, at
> Times, a grand, flamboyant lust.
> (qtd. in Parthasarathy 23)

In her poem "The Invitation," Das longs for the 'right' kind of man. The man she wanted never met her. She expresses her desires in the lines:

> For long I've waited for the right one
> To come, the bright one, the right one to live
> In the blue. No. I am still young
> And I need that man for construction and
> Destruction. Leave me.... (qtd. in Parthasarathy 26)

Thus, the theme of love and sex runs through some of her prominent poems. She creates the picture of love and sexuality not for the sake of playing adultery, but she really wants to rescue from the clutches of male-dominated world. She hopes a happy and healthy life of peace and rest.

Rajagopal Parthasarathy was born at Tirupparaiturai near Trich in 1934. He edited *Poetry from Leeds* and *Ten Twentieth Century Indian Poets*. His *Rough Passage* is only volume of verse appeared in 1977. Though he could not achieve the Commonwealth Poetry Award for 1977, he was highly praised by the judges. He was honoured with the Ulka Poetry Prize, sponsored by Poetry India, in 1966. He is quite different from his contemporaries in terms of his contemporary concern in his poetry. Most of his poetry hovers around the conflict between Tamil culture and the European culture. Like his contemporaries, his poetry seems to be marked with the quest for identity. He himself admits that "He dwells upon the question of language and identity and upon the inner conflict that arises from being brought up in two cultures" (Parthasarathy 74).

In "Exile," Parthasarathy deals with the opposition of the culture of Europe with that of India. The title itself suggests the theme of the poem. He comes to the point that to run after English tradition and culture is baseless, for creativity cannot take shape in alien language:

> He had spent his youth whoring
> after English gods

There is something to be said for
exile:
You learn roots are deep.
That language is a tree, loses
colour
under another sky. (Parthasarathy 75)

The poet always remembers his past and present. Here, he recalls his days in Jadhavpur:

Trees, big with shade, squat in
the maidan
as I walk, my tongue hunchbacked
with words, towards Jadhavpur
to your arms. (Parthasarathy 76)

Parthasarathy describes his experiences in London as useless and fruitless:

Nothing can really
be dispensed with. The heart
needs all
The years have given me little
wisdom,
and give dislodged myself to
find it,
Here, on the banks of the
Hooghly,
in the city job Charnock's
built. (Parthasarathy 76-77)

Thus, Parthasarathy fails to find his home in England. Being dissatisfied in England, his dreams shatter to pieces. The title itself denotes his 'exile' from his own culture and country.

"Trail" depicts concern to human emotions and passions. After dejecting the London life, the poet's persona likes his own cultural perspectives. The poet recalls his childhood attachment:

Over the family-album, the
 other night,
I shared your childhood:
the unruly hair silenced by
 bobpins
and ribbons, eyes half-shut
before the fierce glass,
a ripple of arms round
 Suneeti's neck,
and in the distance, squatting
on fabulous haunches
of all things, the Taj. (Parthasarathy 78)

Parthasarathy seems to be confessing purification of his inner emotions. Being lived in another culture and tradition, a feeling of lacking something is obvious:

> Naturally, where there is an influence of another culture and traditions, something appears to be lacking. One observes the poet's feelings being cut off from the land of his birth. A search outside one's natural environment, on the other hand, gives adequate opportunities to penetrate unfamiliar lands of culture and traditions. Here a feeling of nostalgia pervades. It is something Indian that attracts attention. (Prem 95-96)

The poet accepts Tamil culture with enthusiasm for its unique way of life. "Overwhelm the flight / of human speech / Thus celebrate / something so perishable, trite" (Parthasarathy 80).

"Homecoming," the third part of *Rough Passage* depicts the process of returning to one's home. He thinks that it is difficult to save his culture as he expresses in the state of vulgarity:

My tongue in English
 chains,
I return, after a generation,

to you.
I am at the end
of my Dravidic tether,
hunger for you unassuaged.
I falter, stumble. (Parthasarathy 80)

The poet also shows consciousness about the human relationships among family members. It is supposed that these relations bring happiness and prosperity. The incident of his grandfather's death offers him an opportunity to maintain relation with his family members:

And so it eventually happened—
a family reunion not heard of
since grandfather died in' 59
-in March
this year, cousin arrived in
Tiruchchanur
in overcrowded private buses,
the dust of unlettered years
clouding instant recognition.
Later each one
pulled,
sitting crosslegged on the steps
of the choultry, familiar
coconuts
out of the fire
of rice-and-pickle afternoons. (Parthasarathy 81)

In fact, Parthasarathy attempts to percolate the fair shades of Indian ethos and culture in his poetry from the personal events of his responsibility in life:

> Thus, R. Parthasarathy presents his hopes and aspirations in candid way without touch of irony. The poet's sensitiveness helps him a lot to unfold the tangles of

> human hopes and aspirations. The pain and suffering in exile sharpen the imagination of the poet too much and he comes out as better poet. His presentation of linguistical difficulties with frankness seems to be his great contribution. (Singh 252)

Jayant Mahapatra was born in Cuttak in 1928. He started writing poetry at the age of forty. Otherwise, he is a professor of physics. His poetic works *Close the Sky, Ten by Ten, Svayamvara and other Poems, Countermeasures, Rites, Waiting* and *Relationship* add charm to his poetic achievement. He is honoured with Sahitya Akademi Award for his well known volume *Relationship* in 1981.

Like his contemporaries, he does not cover the vast range of themes. His poetry is marked with local colour which is rare in modern Indian English Poetry. In his poetry, Mahapatra explores the aspects of Indian life in Odisha and the Jagannath Temple of Puri. It renders a pious and religious colour to his poetry. He is original poet as his poetry shows no impact of English poets. He tries to present various aspects of human relationship. His poetry reveals cultural ethos of Indian life through the themes of love, sex and distorted human emotions and passions:

> Jayant Mahapatra is quite modern in his exploration of various tangles of human life. Love, sex, sensuality, poverty, backwardness and religious orthodoxy are some of his important themes which the poet reveals in his poems with ironic detachment. (Singh 187)

Jayant Mahapatra presents the authentic picture of the Jagannath Temple at Puri. He depicts the situation of the widow women who are aged and dressed in white colour and waiting for the entrance into the temple:

> White-clad widowed women
> past the centres of their lives
> are waiting to enter the Great
> Temple.

Their austere eyes
stare like those caught in a net,
hanging by the dawn's shining
strands of faith. (Mahapatra 21)

Thus, the women are caught in the quagmire of orthodoxy and blind belief. In his poem again like Ramanujan, Mahapatra watches the loaded barge floating across the water of the river. The lines express his depth of observation and power of imagery:

The same river, the same sun, the same town.
out of the corner of my eye
the barge loaded with golden hay
trapped like a leaf in a basin of water. (Mahapatra 25)

Indian sensibility is exposed in his poem "Taste for Tomorrow." Mahapatra creates living characters of the priest, the beggar, the fisherman, the crow and puts forth their objective reality. These are the vignettes of Puri symbolizing reality:

At Puri, the crows.
The one wide street
lolls out like a giant tongue.
Five faceless lepers move aside
as a priest passes by.
And at the street's end
the crowds thronging the temple door;
a huge holy flower
swaying in the wind of greater reasons. (Mahapatra 35)

Mahapatra senses the pathos of woman's life in his poetry. He deals with the pathetic condition of woman and also portrays them in all shapes and figures. The emphasis appears in presenting women as the sufferer. In his poem "Indian Summer," he exposes the depressing state of a woman:

The good wife
lies in my bed
through the long afternoon
dreaming still, unexhausted
by the deep roar of funeral pyres. (Mahapatra 39)

"A Missing Person", depicts a woman who is watching for her lover in the "darkened room", and fails to find her "reflection in the mirror":

In the darkened room
a woman
cannot find her reflection in the mirror
waiting as usual
at the edge of sleep
In her hands she holds
the oil lamp
whose drunken yellow flames
know where her lonely body hides. (Mahapatra 89)

Indeed, Mahapatra speaks of humiliation of woman in India. He also speaks of the breaking up of the relationship between man and woman:

> An Indian by heart, he has employed many recurrent Indian themes in his poetry which range from grass-root level problems faced by common man and woman to the corrupt Indian political system. Jayanta Mahapatra is a poet of human relationship raising his situations from the microcosm of Orissa, India to represent the macrocosm of the world. In his poetry, the human relationship centres round man-woman relationship. (M. Sharma, K. Sharma and Mishra 394)

Mahapatra is the poet who sincerely explores the scenes and sights of Orissa. He is oriya to the core. He describes a scene in his poem "Myth" where he is humiliated while trying to enter the famous Hindu Temple with a hope to worship the God. The poem artistically reveals Mahapatra's feeling of rootlessness in his own land. He must have convinced himself by remembering the devotion and sacrifices made by his ancestors in the glory of Orissa's cultural heritage. But the Priest gave his feeling a terrible blow. Therefore, the poet earns for his identity:

> The stairs seem endless,
> lifelong,
> and those peaks too, Annapurna, Dhaulagiri;
> uncertain, impressive as gods.
> I dare not go
> into the dark, dank sanctum
> where the myth shifts
> swiftly from hand to hand, eye to eye.
> The dried, sacrificed
> flowers smile at me. I have become;
> a diamond in my eye.
> Vague grieving years pit against the distant peaks
> like a dying butterfly
> as a bearded, saffron-robed
> man asks me, firmly:
> Are you a Hindu? (Mahapatra 53)

Mahapatra tries to show his closeness to the land in other way. He expresses his relationship with his motherland in his poem "Relationship". He recalls architectural wonder of the Sun Temple of Konaraka, in Orissa and now laments over its gradual ruin in the lines:

> So through this door, through
> the gleaming skin of the three kingdoms
> the mineral, vegetable, and animal,
> to experience the fever of love
> and the deeper undulation of the earth. (Mahapatra 70)

The poet also maintains the balance between various ups and downs of human life. He explores it by saying that the majestic weight of the mountain is balanced by the depth of the hills:

> Late in the evening of life
> an embarrassment prevents
> the world from speaking.
> Can the wide valley here down
> below
> lessen the mountain's weight? (Mahapatra 94)

In fact, Mahapatra is one of the greatest Indian poets writing in English today. His poetry reflects Indian ethos and culture. In Short, his poetry is a sharp voice at the constructive vision of life. Its main concern is human suffering and predicament. It attempts to study human existence in relation to suffering. Thus, the poet offers kind efforts for the betterment of life:

> His sensibility is essentially Indian. But he does not create the impression of Indianness by bringing in such traditional items as tigers, snakes, snakes charmers, jugglers, crocodiles etc. He is really Indian, because he does not consciously try to be Indianness is seen at its best in his poems about Orissa, where the local and the regional is raised to the level of the universal. (Deshraj 2)

Keki Nasserwanji Daruwalla is certainly one of the major voices in Indian English poetry. He won the Sahitya Akademi award. His verse volumes are *Under Orion, Apparition in April, Crossing of Rivers, Winter Poems, The Keeper of the Dead,* and *Landscapes*. He writes with obvious Indian elements having realistic vision of human life. He served as a Police officer for long and as a result his poetry reflects different kind of understanding for the human emotions. His personal observations are not fully facts; they are amalgam of myth and reality. His use of myths is unique for they are an outcome of his observations and extensive consciousness on environment. Union of the nature and human passion is distinctive in his poetry.

Daruwalla, like Nissim Ezekiel, A.K. Ramanujan and Arun Kolatkar, uses many symbols and images from nature and landscape. His sense of landscape is catching for bringing out the beauty of the places along with the reality of the environment. He portrays the landscapes in words so skillfully that it appears rooted in his land. He himself says:

> My poems are rooted in landscape, which anchors the poem. The landscape is not merely there set to the sense but to lead to an illumination, it should be the eye of the spiral, I try that poetry relates to the landscape, both on physical, and on the plane of the spirit. (Daruwalla, *Two Decades of Indian Poetry: 1960-1980* 21)

Daruwalla really brings his experiences as a police in his poetry. The poet gives minutely the picture of socio-political portrayal of the contemporary India. In his most famous poem "Curfew in a Riot Torn City," Daruwalla describes communal violence in social life:

> the starch on your Khaki back
> torns soggy, the feel of things is queer
> You wish to forget it all
> the riot, the town, the people
> that mass of liquefied flesh
> seeking in fear. (Daruwalla n. pag.)

The poet tries to portray picture of riot and curfew. He also highlights the things used in communal riots as weapons like sirens, warrants, lathi blows, soda bottles and acid bulbs. In his another poem "Monologue in a Chambal Valley," the poet puts the truth that economic imbalance, injustice and exploitation give birth to robbers and bandits. These consequences are equated in the lines:

> the mud in your house has changed to sandstone
> the window thatched with khas

and camels work your Persian wheel.
They pay your percentage, I am told
cattle-theives and brothel-owners
and rice-smugglers, lest you have them caught.
(Daruwalla n. pag.)

Daruwalla's "Rumination at Verinag," is a well-known poem for the mythical reference of the union of *Shiva* and *Parvati*. The poet remembers his experience of love and human passion for sex:

I too struck home and the waters of your body rose to engulf me.
We came here in the late summer of our love, the sky above
blue and benign. Your hair trailed over my face and pieced together the bruised
bits of my being. No rheumatic heart ailed me,
but the soul's gout. (Daruwalla *CP* 206)

The poet is also known for his use of artificial mode to describe natural beauty. He denotes the relationship between the sea and the sky with the help of the image, concave mirrors:

The sea and the sky, two concaves
mirroring each other
two giant wings of a purple moth,
a rose-pink oar / looking for a boat,
a lilac axe-blade looking for a tree line.
(Daruwalla *CP* 194)

The poet depicts the scenic beauty of seascape with its various moods. He creates the picture so vividly that the scene appears alive before the eyes of the readers.

Daruwalla's "Fire-Hymn" reveals his religious stand point in a realistic manner. His images present the picture of burning *ghat* in an authentic manner:

The burning ghat erupted
phosphorescene:
and wandering ghost-lights frightened
passers-by
as moonlight scuttled among the
lones. (Daruwalla *CP* 96)

Again most of his images convey the fear of violence, death, and destruction. The poem "Boat-Ride along the Ganga" is based on the reality of the river Ganges. The river Ganga in Hinduism stands for a mother, a life giver, and a goddess. In fact, Daruwalla, views it differently and states the sad side of the river. He observes death, disease and staleness on its bank. While riding upstream on a motorboat, the *ghat* appears him:

slowly the ghat-amphitheatre unfolds
like a diseased nocturnal flower in a dream
that opens its petals only at dusk.
palm-leaf parasols sprouting like freak-mushrooms
brood over platforms that are empty. (Daruwalla *CP* 97)

The poem "Vignette-II" presents the rituals and sacred rites take place on the banks of river Ganga. He refers the river "a soundless interior monologue". The poet gives the description of both the nature and myth:

You go the rounds of the *Panchtirath*
starting from the ghat where Durga
had dropped a sword
to where she dropped an earring
and the Panchganga Ghat where four rivers
are said to meet the Ganga,
like this river of faith going down
the stone-steps to meet the river. (Daruwalla *CP* 101)

Daruwalla, in the poem "The Round of the Seasons," gives the description of every season in India. Moreover, the poem reveals the impact of the seasons on the lives of the people in

India. He also explains his personal experience of love in those seasons. The spring season, *Vasanta,* the season of flowering, celebrates the common superstitious beliefs in India. The season commonly relates with the flowers like *Asoka, Bakala* and *Tilaka*.

In the same poem, the poet calls the spring season as "season for Illusions," because during this time even the natural things do not appear as they are:

> It is the season for illusions:
> night mists turn to drawn haze.
> The scent of the mango-blossom is there
> but not the mango-blossom.
> A bird alights on the leafing lotus bed
> thinking it is an island. (Daruwalla *CP* 210-11)

Daruwalla also describes the season *Grishma* (summer) in the same poem. The summer deals with the heat of the sun, through the mythical figure *Kama*, the God of lust. In this season, *Kama* wants to be cool:

> Kama, in this torrid summer
> Let some things remain cool:
> Her eyes, reflecting the waters,
> The smell of jasmine in her hair,
> Her body dripping with the cold river
> As she steps out on the ghats. (Daruwalla *CP* 211)

Indeed, Daruwalla's poetry describes vividness in nature along with the human passions. He seems to be an architect of Indian landscape and human life. He always attempts to evoke a meaningful harmony in Nature and Man:

> Daruwalla's mind is continually busy in establishing meaningful relationship between Nature and Man, in various ways and in different contexts and it is on the working out of these relationships that the success and failure of these poems would appear to hinge. (Naik, "Landscapes and Inscapes" 65)

In fact, Daruwalla reveals the shades of Indian ethos and culture through the various images of the landscapes. It is his observation which provides him a big scope to highlight the vivid shades of the Indian society. In this respect, his poetry evokes realistic approach of Indian life.

Dom Moraes was born in Bombay in 1938. While he was a student, he won the prestigious Hawthorndon Prize at Oxford in 1958 for his first collection *A Beginning*. It is really arresting that Dom Moraes is the first and youngest non-English poet to get this honour. His other works include *Poems* (1960), *John Nobody* (1965) and *Absences* (1983).

The study of Moraes' poetry is interesting for its elegant and hypnotic imagery. The lyrical beauty and technical virtuosity are the hallmarks of his poetry. It enthralls readers to a mesmerizing world of passion, romance, fear, grief, and death. The surreal textures of his poems weave together a variety of themes—love and war, friendship and alienation, myth and religion. Moraes' poetry has affinities with English romanticism and surrealism represented by Dylan Thomas and George Barker. Jerry Pinto said, "He covered wars, won prizes, loved a series of women and wrote some bloody good poems."

Like Nissim Ezekiel and Kamala Das, Moraes has evolved confessional attitude in his poetry. His confession has no single motive, but it has symbolic implications too. In "A Beginning," his idiom is rooted only in his imagination. The very first poem, about a piper losing his children, is unique, "Even their voices went away / And left an absence: glitter of loss".

Therefore, absence, departure displacement, invasion, exile, loss are key themes of his poetry. In his poems, he describes the isolated child, hurt and confused; the young outsider in England, making up for his insecurity by his dazzling presence; the solitary exile, steering among the illusions and uncertainties of belonging.

However, Moraes seems to be indulged in weaving different threads in his poetry than that of his contemporaries:

> Dom Moraes is quite different from his contemporaries in terms of theme and style both. Dom Moraes has covered a wide range of themes in his poems but he does not take any interest in contemporary events. He has shown total indifference towards contemporary themes. He compensates this lackness by making his flight from personal to general. He expresses the alienation, depression, conflict of head and heart in his poems. He has also described human failures and disillusionment in characteristic manner. His poems cannot be put in certain trends; he encompasses various themes and topics in his poems with effective techniques. (Singh 26)

Arun Kolatkar was born in Kohlapur, Maharashtra in 1932. He received his education in Bombay where he worked professionally as a commercial artist. He is a bilingual poet writing in both Marathi and English. His poetry is about the region in which he has been brought up. His first collection of poems *Jejuri*, published in 1976. He received the Commonwealth Prize in 1977 for his *Jejuri*. It is a collection of poems mainly describing the very essence of rural India especially of Maharashtra. As Deshraj puts:

> He speaks at length of the temples, Indian God Khandoba (i.e. Lord Vishnu), Streets of Bombay, urchins, pilgrimages to Khandoba's temple, myths, legends, bus-stops, priest, importance of sun in Hindu religion etc. "Jejuri" is a long in thirty-one sections. Kolatkar expresses what he sees with the eye of a competent reporter in a language that is colloquial and spare. The result is a poem of unexpected beauty and power. The main subject for his poetry is the nature and involvement in the Indian context celebration of difference and the exploitation of ethnicity. Its structure is as much symbolic as mythological and naturalistic. (6)

Kolatkar's well-known collection in Marathi "Arun Kolatkarchya Kavita" was published in 1976 and got the famous H.S. Gokhale award in 1977. He contributed his time in experimentation in terms of theme and style. He exposes Indian attitude in his poetry. "The Boatride" is a poem noticeable for the poet's sense of feeling towards a series of images. The speedboat symbolizes the journey full of tension and turmoil. He also draws the image of harbour:

> the speedboat swerves off
> leaving behind a divergence
> of sea
> and the whole harbor all
> that floats must burnt
> the sail-boat
> hurl its hulk over
> burly rollers
> surmounted soon in leaps
> and bounds. (qtd. in Parthasarathy 43)

The poet presents the human relationship which is the basic element of human culture and is based on the faith, proper understanding and mutual respect. The wife's disappointment is described in an authentic way:

> his wife has dismissed
> the waves like a queen
> a bond of oiled
> acrobats
> if her shuttered eyes
> move in dark circles
> they move against her will
> winds like the fingers. (qtd. in Parthasarathy 44)

Indians have strong faith in religion. They believe in God and fatalism. They think that God is present everywhere, even they find his presence in stones. The poet has personified stones as some God in his poems. Arun Kolatkar projects Indianness and philosophy in his poetry. His poem "An Old Woman" portrays an old beggar woman who sits outside the temple asking for fifty-paisa coin as alms. The poet presents Indian attitude of a typical beggar who cling to people and harass them until receives the alms:

An old woman grabs
hold of your sleeve
and tags
   along
She wants a fifty paise coin.
She says she will take you
to the horseshoe
   shrine.
You've seen it already.
She hobbles along anyway
and tightens her grip on
   your shirt.
She won't let you go.
You know how old women are.
They stick to you
   like burr. (qtd. in Parthasarathy 49)

Here the poet emphasizes the typical attitude of an old woman who considers begging as her only way of earning for survival. As the poet shows unwillingness to give a fifty-paisa coin, she says, 'what else can an old woman do / on hills as wretched as these?' But suddenly something happens; the poet looks at the sky and finds:

And the hills crack.
And the temples crack.
And the sky
   falls

with a plateglass clatter
around the shatterproof crone
who stands
  alone.
And you are reduced
to so much small change
in her hand. (qtd. in Parthasarathy 50)

Then the poet thinks about the inevitability of fate. The time changes everything—crack hills, crack temples and falling of the sky. At this, the poet feels himself as unimportant as the small coins which are collected by the old woman.

Arun Kolatkar in his poem "Makarand" explains the significance of honey while worshiping God Khandoba. Honey is used as a ritual in bathing the God. Here the poet narrates the worshipping style of the human being in an ironical manner:

Take my shirt off
and go in there to do the
  puja?
No thanks.
Not me
But you go right ahead
if that's what you want
  to do. (qtd. in Parthasarathy 51)

Another poem "Chaitanaya" refers fifteenth century Bengali saint who is suppoed to be the incarnation of Lord Krishna. The poet presents the stones of Jejuri as sweet as grapes. He also shows that every stone in Jejuri is capable of producing some energy and is almost a God in itself:

'Sweet as grapes
Are the stones of Jejuri',
said Chaitanya.
He popped a stone
in his mouth and spat out gods. (qtd. in Parthasarathy 50)

In his poetry, Mahapatra refers Lord Jaggannath, whereas Kolatkar speaks of Khandoba. Both Gods are the incarnations of same Lord Vishnu, the ruler of the universe. Both the poets use some of the dominant issues of their regions. Thus, their poetry is rooted in Indian environment percolating its ethos and culture.

Shiv K. Kumar was born in Lahore in 1921. He served as a professor of English at various colleges and universities. He is a highly reputed and qualified Indian poet writing in English. He is a versatile writer. He is a poet, critic, novelist, short story writer and a playwright. His contribution as a poet in Indian English poetry is unique. During his lifespan, he published many volumes of poetry. *Articulate Silences* (1970), *Cobwebs in the Sun* (1974), *Subterfuges* (1976), *Wood Peckers* (1979) and *Trapfalls in the Sky* (1986) are his verse volumes. As a modern poet, Kumar handled various aspects of modern life in his poetry. He shows great faith in Indian culture and tradition. "His themes are varied—poverty ("Rickshaw-Wallah"), unrequited love ("Waiting") and the theme of cultural interaction, but it is his preoccupation with unhappy sexual love that looms large. The rawness and intensity of feelings gives it a force" (Abidi 268).

Shiv K. Kumar's "Indian Women" is a best poem for giving an authentic picture of a woman. He describes Indian women as the silent spectators of the pain and suffering caused by the religious, traditional and orthodox society. The poet says, "In this triple-baked continent / women don't etch angry eyebrows / on mud walls" (qtd. in Parthasarathy 54). The poet taking the side of women asserts that they absorb the pain mutely without raising voices against the humiliation. They have got poor fate to suffer and remain confined in the mud walls. The poet again expresses the ethos of Indian women:

> Patiently they sit
> like empty pitchers
> on the mouth of the village well

pleating hope in each braid
of their Mississippi-long hair
looking deep into the water's mirror
for the moisture in their eyes. (qtd. in Parthasarathy 54)

The above lines express that like empty pitchers, the women wait patiently to fulfill their desires. They see their tears in water's mirror with a genuine hope. Thus, Kumar brings out the cultural ethos of Indian woman in his most of poetry.

The theme of love, sex and marriage occurs at top position in his poetry. But, the poet shows the importance of sex to maintain the relationship between man and woman. The poet says that sex is spontaneous and intuitive:

It was as though a wild kitten's
padded forepaw had touched off
A single log
of hunger. (qtd. in Satish Kumar 219)

The poet also explores the postures of sexuality in The Sun Temple of Konark. These sexual postures displays act of sex between man and woman. "These stones have wings / and darkness here flaps / into phosphorescene" (qtd. in Satish Kumar 219). Thus, the poet asserts the significance of love and sex in man-woman relationship.

Shiv K. Kumar gives vent to religious and traditional aspects in his poetry. In his poem "Pilgrimage," he focuses on the practices of some religious people. Being not understood the true spirit of the religion; some people try to attract more people to join their religion. A focus is obvious in the lines:

Not all of us spoke the same language–
some coward under the sun's threats
and the dwindling supplies,
others felt amused
at the enforced equalities. (qtd. in Parthasarathy 55)

The poet ponders over the purity and piousness of the river Ganges in an ironical way in his poem "Days in New York":

They wouldn't believe it here
that Ganges water can work miracles:
in spite of the cartloads
of dead men's ashes and bones–
daily offerings to the river. (qtd. in Parthasarathy 56)

The poet tries to draw his attitude towards cultural interaction. He points out the differences between two cultures. His poem "Days in New York," brings forth the cultural plurality. Instead of presenting the cultural conflict, he speaks of the one whole universe. He thinks that the nature of man cannot change. He pictures his life in a different land:

Here I live in a garbage can.
The pile grows bigger each week
with the broken homes
splintered all around.
A black cat chases a shadow
down the passageway:
its whiskers presage another snowstorm.
(qtd. in Parthasarathy 56)

In the following lines, the poet reflects Indian attitude in a different climate:

I open each morning my neighbour's Times,
whisked away from his door
before he sits.
Gloved hands leave no fingerprints.
And a brisk review of
all our yesterdays is no sin. (qtd. in Singh 179)

In India, there is a tradition of reading a newspaper from neighbor's house. This attitude of Indians cannot be changed if put him in any cultural climate.

Shiv K. Kumar's "A Mango Vendor" depicts the predicament of a beautiful woman who sells mangoes on the pavement. She is poor but beautiful. The poet captures the passionate attitude of an old man who is attracted at the beauty of the woman. The woman boldly faces the old man. She says:

> Buy, something, man
> or move on
> to the crypt
> where death will pull
> the remaining stray hair
> from your green skull. (qtd. in Singh 174)

In short, Shiv K. Kumar's poetry is rooted in Indian milieu, though he lives abroad. He captures modern as well as traditional Indian moods and attitudes in his poetry:

> Among his contemporaries, he is a versatile genius who occupies the profession of the poetic composition seriously and artistically. His poems are authentic in depicting the distortion, bewilderment and boredom of modern life. Even though he has spent a considerable period of his life abroad, he shows his deep faith in Indian culture and tradition. His poetry is neither confessional nor the expression of alienation. (Singh 167)

Indeed, Shiv K. Kumar's poetry is marked with modern ideas and diction. Through his lyrical quality, he tries his best to reach the characters from the society. He hits the faint shades of Indian ethos and culture through the various themes in his poetry. Therefore, he stands with his contemporaries in following the modern as well as the traditional.

Purushottam Lal's contribution to Indian English poetry is unique for providing proper name and magnitude to Indian English verse. He was born in Punjab in 1929. But his family shifted to Calcutta and he took his education in Calcutta, the city of joy and culture. His verse volumes are *The Parrot's Death and Other Poems* (1960), *Change They Said* (1966), "Draupadi and Jayadratha and other poems" (1967). Besides, his translations are "Yakshi from Didarganj and other poems" (1969), "The Man of Dharma and the Rasa of Silence" (1974) and "Calcutta: A Long Poem" (1977). He also translated Indian Scriptures.

P. Lal is a versatile genius. He is more sensitive to human concern than his contemporaries. He is more conventional and romantic in diction:

> More conventional and romantic in diction and incongruous in imagery, he is not a poet of the stature of Dom Moraes or Ezekiel though he impresses us by the strong note of feeling and rhythm. His poetry presents a new kind of romanticism 'a personal lyrical awareness of the world seen in vividly emotional terms'. (Abidi 260)

Though P. Lal discards the romanticism of the earlier, his poetry shows a great impact of the Indian scriptures and classics.

P. Lal reveals great concern for human nature. Sometimes, he evokes nature and human nature together. His poem "Leaf" presents the four stages of human life in an ironical manner. He builds tradition and modernity together effectively. While delineating four stages of human life, he does not make to remember the *Ashram system*. He presents the first part of life as full of joy and happiness. This merry-making stage of youth is perfectly depicted in the lines:

> At sixteen, glibe of tongue and shy,
> And slave to graint pride.
> Given to grass and stream and sky
> And flesh, erratic guide.
> But, now I am a leaf; touch me
> with the sun: and
> I will laugh. (qtd. in Singh 35)

The second stage is described as the period of responsibility in human life. The third stage is full of boredom where one waits for aspirations and happening. And the fourth stage is the revelation of human beings. It is in this stage, one can understand the facts of human life. The poet describes this stage:

Bright Tree! Bright branches!
  Tree that lives
In the world's secret root,
Scans sky, field and man,
  and gives
Devotion flowers and fruit,
Of you I am a leaf: touch
  me with the sun: and
I will laugh. (qtd. in Singh 36)

P. Lal, creating the various images of flower and bees, expresses the love of time pass between the flower and the bees, but he also presents human love of vigour and vitality. In his poem "Life," he sings of love:

Is a flower of five petals.
Love is the first
Where a lusting bee settles,
Quenching thirst. (qtd. in Singh 37)

Lal's two poems "The Man of Dharma" and "The Rasa of Silence" are basically born from the myths of the Mahabharata:

> Lal is obviously attempting here a poetic statement about the modern human condition, making a symbolic use of a well-known figure from the Mahabharata, and the theory of rasa from Sanskrit aesthetics. However, the symbolism is vague and he attempted re-classification of rasas unconvincing. (Naik, "The Ashoka Pillar: Independence and After" 198)

The poet also translated many poems from Sanskrit classics. His translations appeared more effective than his creative contribution to some critics. He succeeds in capturing the true spirit of the legends and the epics in his translations:

The man I married is the man
  I loved,
On moonwet nights when the

bowers,
Of my virgin days were filled
With the fragrance of jasmine
flowers.
And my virginal heart still
longs
For the days we spend by the
river,
That ran from the Vindhya
mountain, where
We made love, for ever and
for ever. (qtd. in Singh 44)

Thus, Lal presents the episodes from the Indian scriptures skillfully with authentic favour in his poetry. In fact, his translations reveal his own impression:

> P. Lal is a great genius in presenting the various aspects of Indian myths and legends in own unique style. He beautifully combines the sensuousness, morality, ethics and above all, human hopes and aspirations. He practices his own critical theories and he seems to be true to his own words. He handles the mythical and modern themes equally well. He explores human psychology in his own way. (Singh 45)

P. Lal is a versatile genius among his contemporaries in composing poetry. His contribution to Indian English Poetry is outstanding for his blend of the tradition and the modern. It is through this blend, he reflects Indian ethos and culture in his poetry.

Gieve Patel was born in a Persian family in Mumbai in 1940. Like Ezekiel, he does not speak of rootedness. He credited two volumes of poetry—*Poems* (1966) and *How do you Withstand, Body* (1976). In his poems, Patel has shown great sympathy for the deprived class and the downtrodden class of the society. He creates problems of human beings, but at the same time tries to find out solutions to it. His style of realistic approach to the problems of underdogs and underprivileged make him a poet of the public:

> Patel believes that 'if a poem is clear, well thought out, purposive, logical and true, it will have changed something . . . first, in the poet himself . . . because if this does not happen . . . there is no poem' His poems rightly, therefore, try to make articulate, often sardonically, the pains of growing up. (Parthasarathy 85)

Gieve Patel is a medical practitioner by profession and it helps him to dive deep in the psyche of human ethos. In his poem "Naryal Purnima," he celebrates the Hindu festival. In Hinduism, this festival has imminence significance when *Varuna*, a sea-God is propitiated with coconut to mark the end of the monsoon. He describes the festival in plane words:

> Naryal Purnima should be a few days' halt
> Before the second rains begin; the rice
> Sprouted, transplanted, yet doomed to die
> Without a new month's grace of extra water. (qtd. in Parthasarathy 90)

Patel also cares for the cause of the oppressed, underdogs and downtrodden. He is also aware of his identity, though he never tries to reveal a feeling of rootlessness:

> Had I the will to trouble
> I'd be with the others—the driftwood
> Against a blinking sea–
> Their minds profanely focused
> On the wave—pitched gifts.
> Do I sympathize merely with the underdog?
> Is it one more halt in the search for 'identity'?
> (qtd. in Parthasarathy 91)

The poet has deep sense for the oppressed which becomes clear in his poem "Nargol". In this poem, he feels sympathy and kindness for a leprous woman. He never shows a disgust for the disease like other people:

> I am friendly, I smile, I am
> No snob. Lepers don't disgust me. But also
> Tough resistance: I have no money,
> Meet me later,
> My fingernail rasping a coin. (qtd. in Parthasarathy 88)

The poet equally exposes the cruelty of the human beings against the leprosy and the treatment given to the affected people. He is aware of the people who treat badly these patients:

> Cruel, you're cruel
> From a village full of people
> She has chosen me; year after year;
> Is it need
> Or a private battle?
> At the end it is four annas–
> Four annas for leprosy. It's green
> To give so much
> But I am a rich man's son. (qtd. in Parthasarathy 89)

Gieve Patel, in his poem "Servants," gives an account of the pathos of the working community. He expresses their tiredness after work. The day work has a bad impact on their bodies. He presents their ethos:

> Other hands are wide
> Or shut, it does not matter
> One way or other–
> They sit without thought,
> Mouth slightly open, recovering
> From the day, and the eyes
> Globe into the dim
> But are not informed because

Never have travelled beyond this
Silence. (qtd. in Parthasarathy 87)

The poet's main concern is to voice against the humiliation of the oppressed in the hands of the rich. He shows humanity in finding out the solutions on the problems of tormented.

Gieve Patel, thus, points out the ethos of the distorted people in his poetry. His profession of a doctor helps him critically to bring out the agony of the diseased:

> Nissim Ezekiel highly admires his poetry: "Sobriety, balance and a slow, sometimes heavy gravity are the main qualities of Gieve Patel's verse. He is the most precise and calculating of the Indian poets writing in English. His caution and his craftsmanship are sometimes excessive. The concrete clear words, the polished phrasing, the immaculate image all create the impression of a stable strong character exploring familiar territory. .... in place of the inspired flight of imagination he offers a meticulously integrated process of ideas and feelings. We recognize beneath its apparently cold surface much warmth of sympathy and depth of understanding." (Satish Kumar 206)

In fact, Gieve Patel tries his best to reveal the shades of Indian ethos and culture in his poetry through the sympathy towards distorted, diseased and downtrodden.

Pritish Nandy is a prolific Indian English poet. He was born in 1947. He credited more than a dozen collections. His most acclaimed collections are *Of God and Oliver, The Poetry of Pritish Nandy* and *Tonight this Savage Rite*. He is a love poet and his love poetry is marked with modern trends. The theme of love makes him to reflect various shades of human life. His poetry is full of urban ethos, sex and violence, horror and terror and attraction of the modern life. "Pritish Nandy is a prolific poet of quantity rather than quality. He has several collections of verses to his credit. His poetry strikes the note of protest and experimentation in Indo-English poetry" (Abidi 265).

Nandy depicts the anguish of loneliness in love and life. The poet expresses utter grief in love using various images from nature. He says:

We speak what is darkness
  our love is like memory
your eye is the night
  outside us
nothing exists. (qtd. in Singh 292)

He makes a beautiful comparison between man and nature by creating different images:

Rivers that cannot run
bodies that cannot desire
ships that cannot sail
outside us
the wind
tracing footsteps. (qtd. in Singh 292)

The poet describes the city of Calcutta and its history with malice. He shows closeness with the city and its people. He voices the realities of human life in the modern era:

They will pull you down
  from the Ochterlony
monument and torture each
  broken rib beneath
your upthrust breasts they
  will tear the anguish
from your sullen eyes and
  thrust the bayonet
between your thighs
Calcutta they will tear you
  apart JARASANDHA like. (qtd. in Singh 294)

Nandy writes about love as a thing of faith and value. Love is hopeless without faith and value. The poet sings the melody of love here:

This
parabole is again
love a question of
values, of confusing
principles that guide
our actions at every
stage as lilacs
convert prayer to
love and the city
burns within your
eye. (qtd. in Singh 297)

Thus, the poet gives the experiences of modern man's life in a straightforward way. His observation of life is real and minute.

Gauri Deshpande is another Indian English poet with an outstanding contribution to the poetry. She was born in 1942 and educated at Poona. Her few collections of verse includes *Between Berths* (1968), *Lost Love* (1970) and *Beyond the Slaughter House* (1972). Gauri stands next to Kamala Das for her poetry is full of love, sex, death, loneliness and loss. She expresses womanly feeling throughout her poetry.

However, Gauri Deshpande is a gifted artist for composing poetry from the commonplace:

All the time that day in June
I shivered
A deep foreboding in my guts
Made my breast-tips quiver
(As though the long weaned child
Thirsted again for a flow of milk)
And I felt exhausted by the long walk to the kitchen.
(qtd. in Satish Kumar 305)

Deshpande presents a domestic picture of a family with usual frustration and sadness. In her poem "The Female of the Species," she expresses feminine feeling in a domestic situation:

You sit with them and talk.
She sews and you sit and sip
and speak of the rate of rice
and the price of tea
and the scarcity of cheese.
You know both that you've spoken
of love and despair and ungrateful children.
(qtd. in Prem 336)

Thus, she exposes the domestic problems in India with perfect observation. She, too, expresses a feminine anguish in her poem "The Guest":

You are gone now
The perfect mouth that kissed my words
no longer by
And as the clouds heap and heap upon the west
I lie empty, barren and bereft, (qtd. in Abidi 315)

Again, the poet has a genuine sensual feeling about love and sex:

One moon-month after you left
(I know it by my womb's staining blood)
returns that exact
mist-smudged day of silence and late sun
which had decided what
I shall do without; (qtd. in Abidi 316)

Like Kamala Das, Gauri Deshpande writes about the feminine anguish. She is bold and candid in her expression. On the other hand, she reveals her attachment with her family. Her awareness of the welfare of the family shows her meaningful existence of life:

> Gauri Deshpande speaks of affection and compassion a woman nurses. Her undivided concentration, occupation and anxiety about the welfare of the family and close relations determine her meaning of existence in life.

> The poet appears to express a belief that a woman has a definite purpose and it is she who makes home a worshipping place—a temple. If she is loved and revered, all pains and deprivations disappear. (Prem 335)

Thus, Gauri Deshpande perfects the cause of woman's feeling and reflects Indian ethos and culture in her poetry. But her contribution seems to be captured by the stance like that of Kamala Das; she has painted the cultural ethos of woman in random poems.

Indeed, more than hundreds of poets contributed in Indian English poetry in post-Independence era. But a few of them published their poetry. And very few of them came into the light of intellectual qualities. The select poets of the era are Nissim Ezekiel, A.K. Ramanujan, Kamala Das, R. Parthasarathy, Jayant Mahapatra, K.N. Daruwalla, Dom Moraes, Arun Kolatkar, Gieve Patel, Pritish Nandy, Gauri Deshpande and many others.

Critically speaking, a sense of social awareness lack in the poetry of many Indian English poets:

> Notwithstanding the fact that contemporary poetry is dominated by the trend of personal theme, the charge that new poets are not concerned with contemporary reality is untenable. True, they are not the harbingers of social change but their poetry is not without what is called social awareness. The theme of poverty, social injustice and exploitation has been taken up by many poets in random poets. It is, however, not a recurrent preoccupation. (Abidi 259)

In short, among the poets who reveals a social concern with Indianness and makes it a perfect preoccupation throughout almost all his poetry is Nissim Ezekiel and a few others. "Social awareness is found in the poetry of Nissim Ezekiel, Gieve Patel, Pritish Nandy, Saleem Peeradina and A.K. Mehrotra" (Abidi 259).

The above discussion of Indian English poetry makes to understand that major poets of post-Independence era along with Nissim Ezekiel try their best to come in terms with Indian ethos and culture in their poetry, but most of them have touched the concern in random poems. It is, however, not a recurrent preoccupation of the concern seen in their poetry. To say, Nissim Ezekiel's poetry reveals a recurrent preoccupation of Indian ethos and culture in his poetry with the exception of few poems. In this respect, Bijay Kumar Das points out:

> Ezekiel, unlike Jayant Mahapatra, R. Parthasarathy, A.K. Ramanujan and Kamala Das, does not make an effort to acclimatize an indigenous tradition to English language. Instead, he seeks to relate himself to the contemporary India. Typical Indian beliefs, situations and contemporary society attract him most and he creates a new kind of poetry in Indian English idiom. For instance, his well known poem "Night of the Scorpion" is typically Indian in its theme and its execution is befitting to the theme. (18)

In fact, Nissim Ezekiel's *Very Indian Poems in Indian English* are written with the stance of societal aspect in which he brings out the characteristic Indian attitude. He depicts their ways of speaking English and at the same time a patriotic theme runs in this poetry. This note of social reform cannot be observed in the poetry of contemporary poets. His other poems like "Night of the Scorpion" and "The Visitor" really bring forth his concern with Indian superstitions and blind beliefs. Thus, Ezekiel to some extent excels most of his contemporaries in order to give the transparent reflection of Indian ethos and culture in his poetry.

Works Cited

Abidi, S.Z.H. *Studies in Indo Anglian Poetry.* Bareilly: Prakash Book Depot, 1978, 260-316. Print.

Daruwalla, Keki N. *Collected Poems 1970-2005.* New Delhi: Penguin Books, 2006, 96-211. Print.

________. "Introduction." *Two Decades of Indian Poetry: 1960-1980.* New Delhi: Vikas, 1980, 21. Print.

Das, Bijay Kumar. *The Horizon of Nissim Ezekiel's Poetry.* New Delhi: B. K. Publishing Corporation, 1995, 18. Print.

Das, Kamala. "I have Lived Beautifully." *Debonair* 5.3 (15 May 1974): 41. Print.

________. *Summer in Calcutta.* New Delhi: Everest Press, 1965, 52-55. Text.

Deshraj, Anupama. D. "Ingenuity and Indianness in the Works of Jayanta Mahapatra and Arun Kolatkar." *The Criterion: An International Journal in English* 4.3 (Dec., 2012): 2-6. Web. 21 June 2016.

Dwivedi, A.N. *Kamala Das and Her Poetry.* New Delhi: Atlantic P. and Distributors, 2011, 23. Print.

Gupta, Ramesh Kumar. "A.K. Ramanujan: A Poet Par-Excellence." Ed. Basavaraj Naikar. *Indian English Literature* 3 (2002): 1. Print.

Kumar, Satish. *A Survey of Indian English Poetry.* Bareilly: Prakash Book Depot, 2001, 206-305. Print.

Mahapatra, Jayant. *The Lie of Dawns Poems 1974-2008.* New Delhi: Authors Press, 2009, 21-94. Print.

Naik, M.K. "The Ashoka Pillar: Independence and After." *A History of Indian English Literature.* New Delhi: Sahitya Akademi, 1994, 198. Print.

________. "Landscapes and Inscapes." *Kavya Bharti* 1 (1988): 65. Print.

Parthasarathy, R. *Ten Twentieth-Century Indian Poets.* New Delhi: O.U.P., 1976, 3-91. Print.

Prem, P.C.K. *English Poetry in India: A Comprehensive Survey of Trends and Thought Patterns.* Delhi: Authors Press, 2011, 95-336. Print.

Ramanujan, A.K. *Collected Poems.* Delhi: OUP, 1997, 4-111. Text.

Rana, Sunita. "A Study of Indian English Poetry." *International Journal of Scientific and Research Publications* 10.2 (10 Oct., 2012): 1. Web. 15 June 2016. (www.ijsrp.org)

Sharma, Mukul Kumar, Sharma, Kapil and Mishra, Sanjit. "The Marginalized Women in Jayanta Mahapatra's Poetry." *International Journal of English and Education* 3.2 (July 2013): 394. Web. 21 June 2016.

Singh, K.K. *Indian English Poetry After Independence.* Jaipur: Book Enclave, 2006, 26-297. Print.

4 Indian Ethos and Culture in Nissim Ezekiel's Poetry—I

In this chapter, an attempt is made to study the reflection of Indian ethos and culture in the poetry of Ezekiel written in his early phase of life. This phase is marked with his romantic mood and a realistic portrayal of Indian milieu. This is Ezekiel's richest phase as it explores the sensitive themes like superstitions, man-woman relationship, husband-wife relationship, marriages, ethos of Indian woman, ethos of urban life, love and sex etc. In short, contemporary India is mirrored in his early poetry having the shades of Indian ethos and culture. Ezekiel seems to be the critic of Indian society as he has a deep sense of social conscience. "His social conscience can be seen in his poetic cosmos which is full with the poor, the deprived, the oppressed, the down-trodden and the dregs of the society, suffering under different conditions and locations" (S. Patil 1). Secondly, this phase is remarkable because of the publication of his well known poems like "Night of the Scorpion," "Enterprise," "Urban," "A Morning Walk," "In India," "Visitor," "Old Abyss," "To a Certain Lady," "Penitence," "Marriage" and "Love sonnet" etc.

In the present chapter, the study intends to chart out Ezekiel's poetry chronologically, though the canvas of it is full of various themes. In his early phase of poetic career, he credited *Early Poems* (1945), *A Time to Change* (1952), *Sixty Poems* (1953), *The Third* (1959), *The Unfinished Man* (1960), and *The Exact Name* (1965). Though these verse compositions in his early age carry the impression of immaturity, juvenility and imperfection, they give an insight into the poet's expanding sensibility. Until and unless the self of the poet is exposed, how one can reach the output of his works?

It is a fact that the authenticity of work proves when the origin of the poet is rooted in the culture of the land. Ezekiel is called the poet of typical Indian environment. He is an Indian poet having fresh, modern and original approach to Indian society—Indian family life and hypocrisy. His contrast of tradition and modernity, his major themes of sex, love with reference to man-woman relationship, Indian superstitions, blind beliefs and Indian woman are the main concerns which reflect frank and clear shades of Indian ethos and culture throughout his poetry. "Mr. Ezekiel's poetry is mostly satiric doting on the men, women, their manners and behavioural oddities, relationship between the spouses, their sexual preoccupations and the environments through which all the personae in his poetry have to pass" (Joshi 251).

The present book emphasizes the rootedness of Ezekiel in the culture and attempts to come in terms with Indian ethos and culture:

> ..unless art is rooted in the soil, it is bound to be condemned to both superficiality and artificiality.... This Indianness may take several forms and shapes, and may appear in work of art in diverse ways, obvious and subtle—but it is quality which is unmistakably present in the finest works of all Indian writers, whether they write in their mother tongue or in English. Modern India is a synthesis of many cultural cross currents and modern India, in Mulk Raj Anand's words, is conscious of the double burden on my shoulders, the Alps of the European tradition and the Himalaya of my Indian Past. (Naik, "The Indianness of Indian Poetry in English" 33)

It becomes really controversial to think that being born as a Jew, one cannot claim to be an Indian:

> A major Scottish poet recently said to me, at an international poetry festival in Rotterdam. "You're not a real Indian", and my responses was, "No, we've lived in India only 2,000 years." A Jew can never be a 'real' Indian or a 'real' Chinaman. I'd say Parthasarathy and Ramanujan are 'real' Indians. (Anklesaria 44)

In chapter-2 of the book, an attempt is made to discuss in detail the concern. From the discussion, it comes out that on one side Ezekiel seems associated with Indian scenes, while on other he shows outward relations with India maintained only for the sake of writing poetry. In fact, while coming in terms of Indian ethos and culture in his poetry, it is essential to keep in mind this unity of association and disassociation.

Equally, Ezekiel's technique, his employment of imagery, humour, irony as a weapon of satire, his use of free verse and traditional meters, and his use of lucid, clear, simple, colloquial language may be of great help to focus Indian ethos and culture to some extent. Ezekiel's poetry is like a galaxy of many literary aspects, which sparkle the various shades of Indian scenes. Ezekiel seems to be a craftsman of his poetry. Formerly a craftsman often makes the whole of an article himself by hand putting into his work all his skill, all his experience and all his heart. In the same way, Ezekiel tried to decorate his poetry with vivid imagery, humour as a weapon of satire, simple colloquial language, the conflict of tradition and modernism, the city and the village life in India. He equally uses free verse and rigours of metrical verse. "To him poetry is not a gift to be adorned but a craft to be studied seriously. He believes in the revision of a poem and works hard on it, till it achieves a kind of perfection" (B. Das, "Imagery in the Poetry of Nissim Ezekiel" 12).

Basically, Ezekiel has a keen insight and interest in Indian atmosphere and its people. Ezekiel tried to go deep in the water of Indian ocean where he meets number of fish in the guise of human beings having various modes of attitudes reflecting variety of thoughts and behaviour. As Ezekiel's poetry reveals him as a poet of ordinary human situations and common human relationship, the reflection of Indian ethos and culture becomes his main concern, which made him the most outstanding modern Indian poets writing in English.

Many Indian poets like A.K. Ramanujan, R. Parthasarathi, Kamla Das, Arun Kolhatkar tried to handle the issue, but Ezekiel's attempt to capture the Indian ethos and culture is marvellous with a new dimension. Ezekiel's concern is not confined only to describe Indian attitude from the love-experiences like Kamala Das, but he also handled the every aspects concerning to the Indian life.

Ezekiel treats life as a journey in which poetry can be a medium of self-discovery. But in the light of his quest for the true meaning of life, Ezekiel seems to be burdened with the corruption caused due to the trivialities and superficial attitude of the modern world. In *A Time to Change*, the poem "The Double Horror" deals with self-discovery. The image of 'nightmare' is striking. It shows that the world has corruption and as an individual is an inseparable part of the world, he is also infected. Then there is an exchange of corruption between the individual and the world. "Corrupted by the world I must infect the world / With my corruption. This double horror holds me / Like a nightmare from which I cannot wake," (*CP* 8).

"Something to Pursue" is another piece of Ezekiel, which is dedicated to his brother Joe. The opening paragraph expresses the poet's efforts to overcome the tension which is the result of opposites:

> Not constancy, not charity, nor fear
> But as it were, a preparation
> Willingness to come to these.
> High endeavour with intensities
> of feeling and of thought,
> that I may see myself
> No longer unresolved

But definite as morning
Moving to fruition
When the season comes. (*CP* 14)

The lines expose that the poet is interested in a simple life which is the source of happiness. It appears from his early poems that Ezekiel was born to compose poetry. The journey in the search of self-started through the theme of man-woman relationship which predominates in his first volume *A Time to Change*:

> "A Time to Change" is a turning point in the history of Indian English Poetry. By using contemporary urban images, language and concerns Ezekiel brought the skepticism, restlessness, feeling of alienation and quest for some meaning to life that is so much a part of the modern mind. (Mahan 8)

"To a Certain Lady" in *A Time to Change* a well-known poem on the theme of marriage based upon the man-woman relationship clearly expresses Indian ethos and culture. The institution of marriage for procreation of human species has traditional sanction. Ezekiel, a great admirer of this institution, never treats love as an activity free from social censor and religious sanctity. Ezekiel's views about marital life genuinely help to couples as a guideline. In this respect, he proves himself as an Indian English poet and a critic of Indian ethos and culture.

According to him married life is full of quarrels and indifference, but the relations between husband and wife must be maintained at all costs. Love and mutual understanding are necessary for success in married life. Commitments and promises play an important role in married life. Husband and wife are like the two wheels of a bullock-cart and it cannot be run because of damage in anyone. Ezekiel in his poem "To a Certain Lady" clears that compromise makes conjugal life happy one: "Always we must be lovers / Man and wife at work upon the hard / Mass of material which is the world" (*CP* 29). In the same poem, he describes the day-to-day domestic scene of average Indian couple:

Then, absences and quarrels, indifference
Sucking like a leech upon the flesh,
Crude acceptance of the need for one another,
Tasteless encounters in the dark, daily
Companionship with neither love nor hate (*CP* 29)

His "Marriage Poem" is a token of conjugal happiness. The poem believes in marital love to prove it as a blessing. The marriage tends partners to sacrificial love and happiness. The poem gives the attitude of mutual understanding:

Earthly love, O earthly love,
Be active when you will
But let the quieter passion come
To every lover, till
The nuptial pattern is secure
Though you are still. (*CP* 46)

The spirit of compromise is a kind of adjustment in marital life. It hires openness to attitude. The protagonist in "Prayer I" urges the deity for this spirit:

If I could pray, the gist of my
Demanding would be simply this:
Quietude. The ordered mind.
Erasure of the inner lie.
And only love in every kiss. (*CP* 54)

The artificial relationship creates discord between husband and wife which leads both to mental tension. The female persona in "Situation" (*The Third*) "never spoke her mind". Instead of clearing the differences, the partners choose to live in illusion. The sense of despair grips the unfortunate couple:

They did not say a thing to counteract despair.
Nor planned to satisfy the hunger in their eyes.
A little guiltily she smoothed down her hair,
And safe in her affection he told his moderates lies. (*CP* 109)

Ezekiel seems to be the master in sketching the portraits of individual human beings wherein he searches for Indian ethos and culture. From judging others' attitude, he returns to his own psyche. It is his psyche, which compels to think that perhaps he is worried by doubts about his own sexual capacity and never achieves satisfactory relations in extra-marital life. Ezekiel here confesses like that of Kamala Das. The absence of genuine communication in extra-marital sex relation is clearly seen in his poem "An Affair":

> And then she said: I love you, just like this
> As I had seen the yellow blondes declare
> Upon the screen, and even stroked my hair,
> But hates me now because I did not kiss. (*CP* 11)

Ezekiel's treatment of the theme of woman is an epoch making in terms of her ethos and culture. She has been treated in Indian society as a responsible one for all happenings either good or worse. "As a follower of a monotheistic religion—Judaism—Ezekiel shares with brethren of his religious creed the ingrained prejudice against the fair sex as the corruptor of flesh. The entire responsibility of the Fall is attributed to the Woman (Eve) traditionally in Christianity, Islam and Judaism" (S. Mishra 50). In his poem "Old Abyss", the girl who is deserted along with her child from her husband due to her faithlessness becomes the victim of torture:

> This girl, once married, with a child,
> But now alone torments
> The men she knows
> With such magnificence in movement
> (I have died beholding it)
> They see the old abyss again—
> Desire with object near and far. (*CP* 48)

The poet does not stop by using metaphor 'torment' but calls her witchery. She is presented here as an animal and a devil spirit haunting man. Man can redeem only "When the female animal no longer / Haunts the bed in flesh or dream" (*CP* 18). Ezekiel presents her ethos by comparing her to animate and inanimate things and not allowing her equality and evenness in his poem "Conclusion":

> That woman, trees, tables, waves and birds,
> Buildings, stones, steamrollers,
> Cats and clocks
> Are here to be enjoyed
> ....
> The true business of living is seeing, touching, kissing
> The epic of walking in the street and loving on the bed.
> (*CP* 96-97)

In the poem "Penitence", he expresses the tension between powerful passions and a sense of guilt and wishes to be penitent:

> I will be penitent,
> My heart, and crave
> No more the impulse
> of a wave.
> But I am still a sea
> And hold within
> The muffled tumult
> of a sin. (*CP* 71)

Ezekiel seems to be a poet of social issues like degradation of women and her ethos. He comes as a social reformer in terms of woman's ethos like giving her rights equal to man. He wants to repair the social ills for betterment of human life. His poetry raises its voice against social injustice and domestic violence. It compels him to expose the follies and faults of Indians. Thus, Ezekiel proves himself a critic of Indian society and its ethos and culture.

The theme of love, sex and marriage, in Ezekiel's poetry, is the basic of man-woman relationship which genuinely expresses Indian ethos and culture. He does not apply love and sex as a taboo, but as an interpretation of "perennial human tradition". While dealing with the theme of love and sex, Ezekiel explores man-woman relationship from the male point of view. Here he seems an exponent of Indian ethos and culture in his outlook for in male-dominated Indian society woman plays a subordinate role. She performs various parts such as mother, daughter, sister, and wife and perhaps sometimes whore and sex object.

In fact, Ezekiel's early poetry is the outcome of his youth and a beginning of his poetic career. His early involvement in love and sex determines his attitude to life. His frustration and failure in love makes him a man of bitter experiences. As a result, he enthralls himself into the anxieties of life. In this relation Bijay Kumar Das asserts:

> Love, city and self are the major preoccupations of Ezekiel in the beginning of his poetic career. Unrequited love and resultant disappointment dominate the mood of his early poetry. Torment of the flesh and the spirit resulting from the unfulfilled love governs the poet's attitude to life. In such a situation, 'youth runs out of the song' and there is a need 'to start again' for 'love of life can always be renewed'. The desire to come to terms with reality seems to have overwhelmed the poet. Frustration in life resulting out of the failure in achieving one's goal seems to have made the poet a bitter man. His desire to be a successful poet and lover worries him without end. ("The Horizon of Nissim Ezekiel's Poetry" 7)

While handling the theme of sex and love, Ezekiel captures Indian attitude and tries to reach its depth. In this effort, he does not think that he is crossing the boundary of morality. In his poem "Scriptures," he attempts to show oscillation between the rules of morality and the force of temptation. Sometimes people try to wash their hands in Ganges in order to purify their sins as the teaching of Hindu mythology. But as soon as the impact of teaching is released, they yield to temptation: "So we lose the parable again / and are accused again at home" (*CP* 50).

Moreover, Ezekiel is frank and candid in describing sex and woman as sex object. For him woman, is an instrument of enjoyment and her nakedness is a mystery for searching eyes of men as he describes in "At the Party":

> Ethereal beauties, may you always be
> Dedicate to love and reckless shopping,
> Your midriffs moist and your thighs unruly,
> Breast beneath the fabric slyly flopping. (*CP* 98)

Like John Donne and other Metaphysical poets of England, he equally paves way to the physical as well as spiritual love. K.N. Daruwalla rightly remarks: "The themes of departure and voyage, both spiritual and physical, the one complementing the other, and his rodent like explorations of the various aspects of love the celebration of flesh, breakdown of married love, the transmutation of sex to blessedness are recurring motives in Ezekiel's poetry" (qtd. in Kumar 178).

Ezekiel treats the theme of love and sex with an eye of a psychologist. He is also 'a poet of the body' in his *Sixty Poems* and *The Third*. He says that the thrust of body cannot be ignored. It cannot be suppressed for any length of time as expressed in "Nakedness II":

> Then, wanting to be whole again, he prayed:
> That this his body may belong to him
> And let him understand: that in the working
> Of his mind the body takes a hand. (*CP* 61)

Ezekiel's concept of the relation of body and mind regarding sex really makes to think about his philosophical approach. He honestly clears the instinct of the human body and mind: "a poet of the body; and an endless explorer of the labyrinths of the mind, the devious delving and twisting of the ego, and the ceaseless attempt of man and poet to define himself, to find through all 'the myth and maze' a way to honesty and love" (Hess 30).

Like Ezekiel, Kamala Das too deals with the theme of the body in her poetry. Among many Indian English poets, Ezekiel and Das have shown close attachment to body and sex in their poetry. Kamala Das, in her poem "A Relationship," says:

> My body's wisdom tells and tells again
> That I shall find my rest, my sleep, my place
> And even death nowhere else but here in
> My betrayer's arms.... (qtd. in Dwivedi 23)

Sometimes Kamal Das likes her body, but here she seems to be tired of body and sex, while Ezekiel never shows dislike for body and sex:

> Related to the theme of love is the theme of the body in Mrs. Das's verse. Sometimes she likes her body, while at others she dislikes it. Physically, she is 'dark' with ordinary features, and her loathing for the body is mainly due to this factor as well as to her protracted illness. In liking the body, she resembles Nissim Ezekiel, who is also a 'poet of the body'. Both these poets, like American 'Confessional' poets, accept whole-heartedly the demands of the body. (Dwivedi 22)

Ezekiel's poem "At the Hotel" presents the concealed ethos and culture of average Indian. It has been a taboo in India since log time to praise sex and love. Looking into the personal life of Maharajas in India, this practice of keeping woman for sexual satisfaction and prestige was remarkable. Here, the renewal of the same physical cultural ethos is seen in continuation. The poem shows the sexual mission of people to go to parties and hotels:

> Our motives were concealed but clear,
> not coffee but the Cuban dancer took us there,
> the naked Cuban dancer.
> On the dot she came and shook her breasts
> all over us and dropped
> the thin transparent skirt she wore.

Was it not this for which we came?
The noise, the smoke, the smell of flesh we relished
Secretly and wanted more,
we drank our coffee swiftly
when the Cuban dancer left the floor,
the naked Cuban dancer. (*CP* 112)

The man-woman relationship has completely been exercised by Ezekiel but he fails to idealize it. Consequently, sex plays a dominant role and thus the longing for carnal desire is highlighted in many of his poems. V.A. Shahane remarks about his early poetry:

> Ezekiel's earlier verse is marked by an awareness of physical passion, sexual impulse, intermingling of the corporeal and the spiritual and a sensitive reaction to objects of sensory pleasure or pain. The promptings of the spirit are audible. Through the limbs of the flesh and the consequential significance of intellectually and abstraction are obtained and realized only through the emotively stimulating effect of the human body. (22)

Ezekiel's love for nature cannot be ignored while coming in terms of Indian ethos and culture. Indeed, nature has immense importance in Indian cultural ethos. Nature is necessary for fruitful living and the elements of nature are symbolic of ethical values in Ezekiel's poetry:

There is a landscape certainly, the sea
Among its broad realities, attracts
Because it is a symbol of the free
Demonic life within,
Hardly suggested by the surface facts,
And rivers what a man can hope to win
By simple flowing, learning how to flow,
Besides that all organic growth is slow. (*CP* 39)

In his poem "Song," Ezekiel presents blossoms of summer as symbol of prosperity, charity and lucidity which are the aspects of Indian culture: "Charity, lucidity— / Remarkable in the mood of seems / The doom of all my traffic dreams" (*CP* 42).

Rainwater is a traditional symbol of Indian culture and consequently rain brings prosperity in the life of an Indian farmer. Ezekiel, in "After Rain," describes the rain as a symbol of purification of life:

> And so I went, as the weather cleared,
> Walking on the wet road, to know
> If the scene had taken on a novel glow,
> Lamplight, moonlight, dripping branches, wet road
> Purer, sweeter, And now I know,
> It is just so. (*CP* 63)

Ezekiel's skills of presenting blind beliefs must be worshiped in terms of Indian ethos and culture. In India, the elements of nature like storm, thundering, lightning, ghost, some birds like owl, bats are treated as symbols of blind beliefs. In his poem "Occupation" Ezekiel depicts these symbols of blind beliefs:

> It was a stormy scene:
> Thunder, lightning,
> A multitude of ghost among the trees,
> Darkness, cold and restlessness,
> A screeching owl, bats,
> Many strange voices,... (*CP* 24)

Birds like owl and bats are looked upon signs of bad omen in Indian society. The black bird 'crow' is also looked down upon and considered as a messenger of *Yama* (God of death) in Hinduism. In "The Crows", the poet expresses contempt and displeasure at the cry of this bird:

> I hear them from my narrow bed,
> I do not love, I only fear

Their cries of hidden duty's word,
Unwelcome, loud, funereal bird. (*CP* 41)

Ezekiel presents nature as a symbol of purity and tranquility. Nature for Ezekiel is a guiding aspect to seek truth in life. In his use of imagery from the object of nature, he searches the past ethos and culture of India. In *A Time to Change*, the poet recalls "new orchids or unimagined seas", and "discovery of cities fresh as brides". In "A Word for the Wind," the poet considers the wind as a source of inspiration. In "Stone," the poet finds consolation in the objects of nature and makes himself a worshiper of nature exactly like that of William Wordsworth.

Ezekiel's poetry also focuses on his interest in ornithology and natural history. It may confess that animals also have emotions like human beings. They, too, can take interest in the act of making love among themselves. In his poem "Aside", it larks clearly that the animals can be restless for sex like human beings:

One cannot imagine
Elephants making love,
But it seems they do
So also tortoises
And snails,
Or even other men
With women doing
What it seems they do. (*CP* 93)

It is an interesting and realistic observation of the environment by Ezekiel in which he lives. Ezekiel's "The Behaviour of Love Birds," pictures the lustful trails faced by a pair of animals:

The more the female fluffs
the readier she is,
and the more the male is encouraged,
Finally, she solicits copulation
by leaning forward,

raising her head,
and her
  tail.
Newly formed pairs
are rather awkward.
The males make many mistakes,
are frequently threatened
and thwarted
by their mates. (n. pag.)

Ezekiel's visualization of the act of copulation in the world of animals is astonishing to the human minds. It seems that he wants to accept that if animals cannot live without sex, how can human beings. He exposes the fact that carnal desire is natural instinct and man and woman cannot live a happy life without the gratification of sex. In fact, the poet is aware of the elements of nature and its happenings and the eternal reality. He does not only try to bring out the cultural ethos of the human beings, but also that of the other animals on this planet.

In the poem "What Frightens Me," the poet projects the fear in a candid manner. He exposes his personality with introspection and confession of the weaknesses within him:

I have long watched myself
Remotely doing what I had to do,
At times a shamed but always
Rationalizing all I do.
I have heard the endless silent dialogue
Between the self-protective self
And the self naked.
I have seen the mask
And the secret behind the mask... (*CP* 106)

The poet assumes the stance of an observer that an 'observer being observed'. Thus the poet deals with the human weaknesses through the self-observation.

Ezekiel's attitude to religion is rational, secular, logical and humanistic. As in "Psalms 151" he feels:

Deliver me from evil, Lord
Rouse me to essential good,
Change the drink for me, Lord
Lead me from the waiting wood. (*CP* 73)

Ezekiel's "meditative self-explorations" is the result of his desire to pray God, which also turns him towards spiritualism to little degree. In "Morning Prayer" in *The Unfinished Man*, Ezekiel prays to God that mere human emotions are not sufficient to create great poetry unless He grants him ability to compose good poetry. The poet prays to God thus:

Whatever the enigma,
The passion of the blood,
Grant me the metaphor
To make it human good. (*CP* 122)

The piece "Urban" in *The Unfinished Man* is a remarkable poem on the urban theme where the trees appear to him like ghosts losing their personal identity. He employs various images from the objects of nature in his poem "Urban":

The hills are always far away.
He knows the broken roads, and moves
In circles tracked within his head.
Before he wakes and has his say,
The river which he claims he loves
Is dry, and all the winds lie dead.
At dawn he never sees the skies
Which, silently, are born again.
Nor feels the shadow of the night
Recline their fingers on his eyes,

He welcomes neither sun nor rain.
His landscape has no depth or height. (*CP* 117)

These images of hills, rivers, wind, skies, sun and rain represent the polarity to the image of the city. Perhaps, these objects of nature denote ethical values and smooth flow of culture. They have become the archetypal life symbols. As K.D. Verma points out that:

> [T]hey project a pastoral vision of a fully refulgent and harmonious life, a pattern in which man enters into sacred communion with his cosmos including objects of nature as a metaphoric condition of his integrated humanity and of his desire to foster a community of being. (231)

The poem also reminds us the same feeling about the city of London expressed by T.S. Eliot in his poem "The Waste Land". Eliot depicts the degeneration of the society and therefore the city of London has become wasteland. Similarly, Ezekiel states his feeling about the city of Bombay in "Urban":

The city like a passion burns,
He dreams of morning walks, alone,
and floating on a wave of sand.
But still his mind its traffic turns
Away from branch and tree and stone
To kindred clamour close at hand. (*CP* 117)

The poem reflects the changing ethos and culture of the urban man. He is confused without any aim of life, as human desires are never fulfilled. His passion for sex is unlimited. Hence, his degeneration is ultimate. Bijay Kumar Das comments on the poem and the poet:

> As a man strives to exist in a modern urban society, to search for truth and to realize identity with the self and the community his struggles, failures and frustrations reveal not only his own inward nature but also the insufficiency and frailty of the fallen city.... 'Urban' is a very compact poem so far as the imagery is concerned.

> The city that 'like a passion burns' is the image of the bride, and in an ideal sense a complete sexual union would mark the realization of fullness and identity. Since the persona merely 'dreams' and shies away from her, the use of the keyword 'kindred' in the last line turns out to be ironical. Thus what the persona achieves is a kind of illusory union with the 'city' and this forms a kind of habitual response to it. ("Imagery in the Poetry of Nissim Ezekiel" 19)

A.K. Ramanujan too echoes the voice like that of Ezekiel in his poem "A River". Ramanujan narrates the ethos and culture of the historical river *Vaigai* in Madurai. The poet sings the past glory of Madurai, the city of temples and poets:

> In Madurai,
> city of temples and poets
> who sang of cities and temples:
> every summer
> a river dries to a trickle
> in the sand,
> baring the sand-ribs,
> straw and woman's hair
> clogging the Watergates
> at the rusty bars
> under the bridges with patches
> of repair all over them,
> the wet stones glistening like sleepy
> crocodiles, the dry ones
> shaven water-buffalos lounging in the sun.
> (Ramanujan 38)

In fact, Ramanujan shows that the holy river *Vaigai* which flows through Madurai, a city that has history of Tamil culture for about two thousand years. The river remains no more of significance for it carries the hair of woman. The bridge is old full of patches of repair. The water has lost its purity for buffaloes are seen taking rest in it. He creates the images of "wet stones" and "sleepy crocodiles". Therefore, the state of dehumanizing is on the verge.

Bombay has been an inspiring city for many new poets. For Dom Moraes, the city appears a '*cave*' describing its primitiveness and savageness. Gieve Patel is tired with the '*eternal station odour*' of Bombay. The squalor of the metropolis reveals the spiritual decay of human existence. Like Ezekiel, Daruwalla also comments on the ugliness of metropolitan city, Bombay as, "black yeast / from here, and black salt, a wall of rotting muscle" (Daruwalla *CP* 193). Again the Bombay soul full of woodenness is expressed by Daruwalla: "I am the doctor who bangs his doors shut / on a queue of waiting patients" (n. pag.).

Ezekiel brings forth a shift in ethos and culture of city dwellers in the past and the present. It looks that the city of Bombay has become the central figure in modern poetry. It is not only in Ezekiel's but also in Eliot's poetry; the image of city has acquired a proper position and has raised the horizon of their poetics. In his treatment of the image of the city of Bombay, Ezekiel tries to reveal the very Indian ethos and culture of the city dwellers. As he makes some observation in his poem "A Morning Walk":

> Barbaric city sick with slums,
> Deprived of seasons, blessed with rains,
> Its hawkers, beggars, iron-lunged,
> Processions led by frantic drums,
> A million purgatorial lanes,
> And child-like masses many-tongued,
> Whose images are in words and crumbs. (*CP* 119)

The poet not only expressed the degenerated voices of human hearts, but also created other images like slums, hawkers, beggars, processions, drums and purgatorial lanes. Ezekiel depicts the city of Bombay with its ugliness and lacks the historical dimension. The city is as much within him as without: "Ezekiel's originality lies in his perfection of Bombay as a metaphor which defines the alienation of the modern Indian intellectual, brought up in the Judea-Christian and Greece-Roman traditions and being forced to come to life is controlled by a totally different metaphysics" (J. Patil 209).

Kamla Das, too, tired of the city of Bomabay. She feels that the city is a kind of burden on her mind and her personal life is disturbed by its mentality. Therefore, she bids a terrible goodbye to Bombay in her poem "Farewell to Bombay." She says:

> I take leave of you, fair city, while tears
> Hide somewhere in my adult eyes
> And sadness is silent as a stone
> In the river's unmoving
> Core...
> It's goodbye, goodbye, goodbye,
> To slender shapes behind windowpanes
> Shut against indiscriminate desire
> And rain... (K. Das, "Summer in Calcutta" 39)

Das bids farewell with heavy heart to the city of Bombay on the personal basis. Leaving the home of her parents, she makes the city of Bombay her own home with the hope that being loved by her husband. Whereas Ezekiel is got bored of the city of Bombay on the ground of changing mentality and humanity of the city:

> Nissim Ezekiel also is with Kamala Das in expressing his sense of annul and boredom toward the city of Bombay—'The city wakes, where fame is cheap / And he belongs an active fool' ("A Morning Walk"). But in Ezekiel the sense of loss is of a different nature; it is 'depersonalized,' so to say. On the contrary, Kamala *feels acutely* for the loss of her parental home and pure love by making the city as her 'new' home. Coupled with this anguished awareness

> of her loss is her eloquent expression of the pleasures and charms to be found in a big city. (Dwivedi 26)

On the other hand, in fact, Ezekiel, commenting on the city of Bombay, Shirish Chindhade builds the view that Bombay has become the soul of India, for Indians show the acceptance of the city:

> ...Bombay being the very epitome of India in all her minutiae, Ezekiel's poetry has acquired an unmistakable Indian ethos and local colour. There is a profound sense of compassion, understanding, acceptance and sympathy for the city. The poet has seen and known this city in all its aspects. The tone is not one of denigration or denunciation; it is rather, one of understanding and forgiveness. (Chindhade 31)

Indeed, Ezekiel's observation of the city of Bombay though appears like that of T.S. Eliot, it lacks ornateness of British Romantic and Victorian poets. Ezekiel gives a pen portrait of the city. He seems more accurate in presenting the reality of Indian ethos and culture:

> Ezekiel's achievement of freedom from the colonial cringe in poetic art led to more accuracy and realism in the representation of the Indian ethos and milieu in Indian English poetry. Ezekiel focuses his searchlight on the Indian scenario inexorably to accurately perceive and define the reality of the place to which he belongs. He eschews the cosmopolitan universality; he rather concentrates upon his perception of the place, the locale in which he is irrevocably rooted. (Saha 93)

In "Enterprise", the poet makes efforts to reflect the ethos and culture of the Indian society concerning the proverb "diversity in unity". He has made more efforts to establish 'unity in diversity' but he failed due to the tradition-bound attitude of the society. The poem speaks of a group of people who undertake a journey moved by noble aspirations, but it all ends in failure and frustrations, as is usually the case with human attempt at some noble achievement. This happens due to the constituted ethos and culture of Indians, which is exposed in the lines:

> But when the difference arose
> On how to cross a desert patch,
> We lost a friend whose stylish prose
> Was quite the best of entire our batch.
> A shadow falls on us and grows.
> Another phase was reached when we
> Were twice attacked, and lost our way.
> A section claimed its liberty
> To leave the group. I tried to pray.
> Our leader said he smelt the sea. (*CP* 118)

In fact, the group of travellers overcome dangers and difficulties and it makes the journey happy for some time. Soon there are differences of opinion among the travellers. They began to quarrel over trifle things. Their leader feels that they have reached a dead end and thinks to end this pilgrimage.

Ezekiel presents the self-using commonplace but intimate situations. He builds relationship between the urban and the primitive in his poetry. The persona in the poem "Commitment" after failures compels to make self-analysis and lastly reaches to the conclusion to take meaningful action. Actually, without failure one cannot sense of success. Therefore, the poem presents the theme of action as an existential imperative:

> When, with sudden smile, the visions come
> Inviting us to sweet disaster,
> We envy saints their martyrdom
> And press the accelerator. (*CP* 121)

Commenting on the failure, Sanjit Mishra says:

> Disaster can be sweet and welcome only to a man of firm resolve, undeterred by the bending quantum of insurmountable obstacles. Saints achieve their spiritual

> stature through a suffering of infinite proportions without ever betraying any sign of panic in the face of existential hazards. (80)

Again, Indian society's acceptance of the institution of marriage is interesting and the married person is considered fortunate and privileged. Ezekiel's poem "Marriage" describes the couple's journey from the pleasure of innocence to that of experience. The poem takes the traditional view of marriage and creates the scenes of sin and guilt. The poet expresses his own marriage experience of innocence:

> Eternity with touching grace.
> Complacent at being fated
> Never to be separated.
> The bride is always pretty, the groom
> A lucky man. The darkened room
> Roars out the joy of flesh and blood.
> The use of nakedness is good. (*CP* 124)

The poet enjoys the ecstasies of marriage in the beginning and experiences the miseries which come later in lives of both, husband and wife. Thus, Ezekiel experiences the institution of marriage from very near and gives expression to it in his poems. In the next stanza, Ezekiel's innocence results in troubles:

> I went through this, believing all,
> Our love denied the Primal Fall.
> Wordless, we walked among the trees,
> And felt immortal as the breeze.
> However many times we came
> Apart, we came together. The same
> Thing over and over again.
> Then suddenly the mark of Cain
> Began to show on her and me. (*CP* 124)

The poet skillfully brings out the nature of conflict and the closeness in married life. At the same time, he teaches the closeness in married life is not depending on only sexual relations. It gives the idea of guilt in the spouses' psyche for their mere sexual creatures. The dreams shatter to pieces and come out the restrictive nature of marriage. Indeed, Ezekiel's poetry delves deep into Indian ethos and culture through sins and guilt in married life.

Again the poem "Night And Day" discusses the 'ritual of mortality':

> The lovers leave, wives or mistresses
> Put up their hair, restore
> The silk or rayon swiftly shed
> When kisses called the blood
> To act again the ritual of mortality,
> And variously remember.... (*CP* 107)

He considers women with those things which are fragile and best enjoyed from a distance. He also admits that even an emotionless heart is filled with kindness if it possesses a woman.

The Unfinished Man, therefore, escapes from romantic trait that of the first verse-volume. The volume exposes the discontent of apparently settled life. The city of Bombay is the main concern of the poet in *The Unfinished Man*. Bruce King takes note of the poet's successful journey to escape from romantic venture:

> The Unfinished Man is remarkable in its self-scrutinizing psychology and polished craft. The volume moves from generalization towards the personal, from complaint to decision and ideal.... Ezekiel showed how to avoid the excesses of romanticism when writing about the self and its concerns, when making art based on autobiography. (98)

The poem "In India" in *The Exact Name*, gives a picture of the ethos and culture of the native scene. The poem presents a rather wretched picture of India, and its multi-cultural facet having beggars, hawkers, pavement-sleepers, hutment dwellers, slums and others. The poet exposes the city:

> Always, in the sun's eye,
> Here among the beggars,
> Hawkers, pavement sleepers,
> Hutment dwellers, slums,
> Dead souls of men and gods,
> Burnt out mothers, Frightened
> Virgins, wasted child
> And tortured animal,
> All in noisy silence
> Suffering the place and time,
> I ride my elephant of thought,
> A Cezanne slung around my neck. (*CP* 131)

Ezekiel thinks that Bombay is not a city of soul. The people often come to the city for the sake of worldly fame and money:

> BOMBAY IS NOT a holy city. No one comes here on a pilgrimage. No one boasts of having learnt during a short visit how to speak in a softer voice or breathe the purer air of solitude. No, Bombay is not an ancient city of myths and poetic experience. What matters in it more than anything else is success, wealth, power, publicity and awards for achievement. No recognition here of miracles, mystic experience, real prayer instead of religious rituals as mechanical as machines. In the presence of the spirit, the ultimate reality of enlightenment, there is, at best, admiration but rarely an embrace of souls. (qtd. in Anklesaria, "A Fragment found among Nissim Ezekiel's papers" 393)

The second section of the poem describes Ezekiel's childhood experiences of living and studying together with mates of different religious tastes. He experienced loose morals, unabashed boasting and hypocrisy of the Roman Catholics, Anglo-Indians and Islamic boys:

They copied, bullied, stole in pairs
They bragged about their love affairs
They carved the table broke the chairs
But never missed their prayers. (*CP* 132)

It is note making that the poet's mates had tremendous impact of religions. Perhaps, it may result due to inculcation of cultural ethos within them by their parents. At the same time, the boys indulge in misdeeds and prove their earnestness in prayer a meaningless one. The situation shows that Christianity and Islam believe in prayers as a part of Indian ethos and culture. Ezekiel rightly exposes the degradation of religious values:

The Anglo-Indian gentleman
Dark whisky in some Jewish den
With Muslims slowly creeping in
Before or after prayers. (*CP* 132)

The poet spares the majority Hindu community from the act of dishonesty and immorality. But in "Background, Casually," he referred the Hindu community and proved his deep sense of Indian society.

In the third section, the Indian wives from rich, pseudo-advanced families affect advancement but by ethos and culture remain traditional in comparison to western culture. This beautiful combination of modern and traditional ethos and culture really shocks to the aspiration of the readers. Ezekiel describes their traditional attitude and helplessness by contrasting them in good humour with their husbands:

The wives of India sit apart.
They do not drink,
they do not talk,
of course, they do not kiss.
The men are quite at home
among the foreign styles
(what fun the flirting is!)

I myself, decorously,
press a thigh or two in sly innocence.
The party is a great success. (*CP* 133)

The fourth section of the poem ironically states the slavish psychological attitude of an Indian woman where she is attracted by the showy European style of life and closeness "with the English Boss". She discusses art and literature in the first meeting. At the second meeting she gets his boorish lust, which tries to force on her:

The struggle had been hard
And not altogether successful.
Certainly the blouse
Would not be used again.
But with true British courtesy
He left her a safety pin
Before she took the elevator down. (*CP* 134)

Ezekiel draws characters in his poetry from real life. The poem "Virginal" deals with the theme of the predicament of a woman who remains unmarried throughout her life in order to become a spinster. In fact, she tries to derive happiness by leading a life of a virgin. This unusual act of a woman is captured in the lines:

You breathe the bitter air of loneliness,
Pretending that it does not matter when
You close the door and switch the wireless on,
Remote from prospect of the wedding kiss.
You say you do not care, and change your dress
To read a book or write a letter, then
You wait. Perhaps you sigh. The day is done.
Your sorrow as it sleeps denies its loss. (*CP* 138)

Such a woman pretends to be happy enough. But she does not understand that she is deceiving herself by going against the established institution of marriage. The loss of remaining unmarried and walking against the flow is captured in the lines:

> You were not made to live like this, although
> Your face suggests that you are reconciled.
> Its gentle sadness as it slowly grew
> And crushed your liveliness, oppressed me too.
> The universe is much too small to hold
> Your longing for a lover and a child. (*CP* 139)

The speaker laments that her attitude of a spinster denies to herself the pleasures of a married life and the motherhood. The conscious and the sub-conscious feelings of a spinster are displayed in this poem. She is suggested that she has no right to remain unmarried and lead a life of a virgin. It seems an extraordinary poem as far as its theme of unusual decision and the feeling of a spinster is concerned. The theme is unusual because Indian culture does not allow a life of spinster. In India, girls are forced in to marriages at an early age by their parents. While in the west, spinsterhood has become almost an institution.

Again a poem "A Woman Observed" is based on a very simple but different theme. The poem describes a pregnant woman staring at some nude paintings in an art gallery. The woman in this poem is a prude who is shocked by the nudity of the woman painted in the pictures. She is upset to see the nudity of human figures in those paintings. Her expression of dislike is clear on her face. But the poet is wandered to see her expressions:

> .... I am ashamed
> to witness it. The life
> in the woman's belly
> swelling her erotic lines
> depresses me, the seed
> and source denied by this
> expression on her face. (*CP* 140)

The poet thinks of the nudity and sexuality of the pregnant woman, the cause of her pregnancy. Being aware of this fact, the lady has an expression of dislike, on her face, for the paintings. It happens to the poet something troubling. Though the lady has worn a dress, her dress cannot conceal the 'sensual movement' and the swollen 'erotic lines' of her body as observed by the poet:

> I watch her sadly as
> she leaves the place, my eyes
> embracing all that sensual
> movement bursting through the dress. (*CP* 140)

The poet tries to express that the child in her womb is as a result of her own experience of nakedness. Thus, Ezekiel's minute observation of a woman is praiseworthy coming in terms of Indian ethos and culture. Thus, the poet very artistically draws the character from Indian scene for his poetry.

In fact, Ezekiel's poetry shows closeness to the Augustan traits where too much importance is given to the study of mankind:

> His poetical work affirms the Augustan traits 'the proper study of mankind is man'. Obviously, his poetry is an exquisite meeting point of poetic faith and actual life. Like his contemporary English poets like Thomas Blackburn, Thom Gunn, and Philip Larkin, Ezekiel hates the pretension. He grimly laughs at the Indian who give inferior position to women in society. The situation of women in a male-dominated society emerges as a matter of deep concern for him. Enslavement and oppression of 'the second sex,' the low status and discriminatory treatment meted out to them, find a place in his poem, "In India". (S. Patil 3)

Ezekiel's skill should be praised to depict the superstitious practices in India in his poetry. Indian life is full of vivid shades of attitudes wherein various characters play major parts. In

"Night of the Scorpion," the poet enters the very fabric of the Indian's minds and hearts. He describes a situation in an Indian village where the poet's mother is stung by a scorpion. The poem exhibits superstitious practices and performs impressive rituals in which Indian ethos and culture is brought out:

> I remember the night my mother
> was stung by a scorpion. Ten hours
> of steady rain had driven him
> to crawl beneath a sack of rice.
> Parting with his poison—flash
> of diabolic tail in the dark room—
> he risked the rain again. (*CP* 130)

The speaker is a peasant who narrates the entire episode in terms of Indian ethos and culture. It gives the picture of a typical village house having the bags of grain. It was continuously raining for ten hours. This is also a presentation of prosperous state of peasantry because the villagers always depend on rain-water. The poet creates a typical Indian scene and the whole cry of the villagers to minimize the pain of the mother. The peasants act: "The peasants came like swarms of flies / and buzzed the name of God a hundred times / to paralyze the Evil One" (*CP* 130).

Ezekiel reflects the best example of human relationship which is the strongest aspect of Indian village life. As the news spread all over the village, the villagers come like swarms of flies. This also shows the speed of communication and connectedness among them. Indian villagers are ideal for the unity and sense of brotherhood. They believe in God and hope to reduce the agony of the mother by taking the name of God for a hundred times. This clearly reflects the blind belief of the villagers. The situation also reveals the superstitious Indian attitude of the villagers. In short, the poem tries to bring out traditional and superstitious behaviour of illiterate rural folk:

> They clicked their tongues.
> With every movement that the scorpion made

his poison moved in mother's blood, they said.
May he sit still, they said.
May the sins of your previous birth
be burned away tonight, they said.
May your suffering decrease
the misfortunes of your next birth, they said.
May the sum of evil
balanced in this unreal world
against the sum of good
become diminished by your pain, they said.
May the poison purify your flesh
of desire, and your spirit of ambition. (*CP* 130)

The first four lines express the popular superstition among the rural folk that of a scorpion stings a human, its poison moves in the blood of the victim with the movement of the scorpion. Indeed, they voice the deep-rooted superstitious beliefs of birth and rebirth. They think that the poison will burn the sins of the mother in a previous birth; or that the poison will minimize the future misfortunes in the next birth; or that the poison will purify her flesh of desire and ambition. This is "the tradition-bound attitude of the community" (Abidi 293).

On the other hand, the poet's father being a rationalist is compelled to follow the superstition out of his love for his wife:

My father, sceptic, rationalist,
trying every curse and blessing,
powder, mixture, herb and hybrid.
He even poured a little paraffin
upon the bitten toe and put a match to it. (*CP* 131)

The father wonders between rational and traditional world and in hurry follows the conventional method and puts a match to the bitten toe of the mother forgetting that the flame will increase the pain instead of reducing it. Thus, his sarcastic attitude is revealed:

> One of the potent themes of the poem appears to be the contrast borne out by the clash of values-the deep, traditional, immanent superstition of illiterate rural folk belief overwhelms the half-baked, urban educated, rational element represented by the father of the persona and the muted, tongue-in-cheek, sarcastic attitude of the persona himself. (Thakur 74)

Typical attitude of Indian mother is most striking feature of Ezekiel's poetry. He draws the bordering timid and affectionate attitude of a typical Indian mother in the poem. Despite the agony of the poison, the mother cares for her children. She expresses her ultimate affection and love in the lines: "My mother only said / Thank God the scorpion picked on me / and spared my children" (*CP* 131). These last lines have touch of rich cultural and remotely typical of Hinduism. Therefore, Ezekiel, living in a culture and observing for such a long time, its attitudes, beliefs and ethos, no more remain a foreigner or unfamiliar.

It is surprising to think that Ezekiel's alienation itself becomes a source of his poetry coming in terms of Indian ethos and culture. The poem achieves a great value in the hearts of Indians:

> While its thematic richness and its technical finesse make "Night of the Scorpion" one of the finest of modern Indian English poems, another significant aspect of it deserves special mention. It is a poem which only an Indian English poet (even though he is largely alienated from the Indian ethos, for his alienation itself is a source of poetry), could have written, since the experience and the responses to it recreated here are rooted in the modern Indian situation. (Naik, "The Tale is in the Sting" 39-40)

Nissim Ezekiel's keen observation of Indian life and its customs, superstitions definitely expose Indian ethos and culture. His poem "The Visitor" also highlights a common Indian superstition that the cawing of a crow foretells the arrival of some guest. "Down through the ages in Indian culture, people follow this superstition; if a crow caws there is going to be a visitor" (Wesly and Chandra 9). The situation is nicely depicted in the poem:

> Three times the crow has cawed
>
> At the window...
>
> The folk belief that following
>
> The crow a visitor would come. (*CP* 138)

The poet follows the folk belief that the arrival of a guest is certain, as the crow has cawed for three times. The protagonist waits all day for a guest since the crow cawed in the morning. This beautifully explores Indian ethos and culture. However, the poet's observation of Indian life is very sharp and realistic. Ezekiel not only observes urban but also country life as he writes:

> ...I must confess...that I have often personally...carried out exercises in direct observation of poverty and affluence, urban and rural modes of living; perceived and assimilated all things Indian wherever they could be found in India.... (Ezekiel, "What is Indian in Indo-English Poetry". Osmania U. 38)

In fact, Ezekiel's poetry from the volume *A Time to Change* to that of *The Third* displays faint shades of Indian ethos and culture through romantic strain in his poetic personality. "A pronounced feature discernible in poems like "Night of the Scorpion" and "In India" is Ezekiel's initiation into Indian cultural ethos characterized by religious multiplicity" (S. Mishra 94). The love and sex depicted in his poetry is a kind of bless for the young hearts, but it does not mean that Ezekiel has crossed the limit of insulting the values in Indian culture. In poems like "Marriage Poem," "An Affair," and "To a Certain Lady," the poet does not put lot of emphasis on discord until and unless the lovers show mutual understanding and appreciation for each other.

In his poems "The Old Abyss" and "For Love's Record," Ezekiel voices the prejudices against the fair sex and thus brings out the ethos of Indian women in reader's eye. He also discussed the elements of nature as positive symbols and negative as well in the poems like "Song," "After Rain," "Occupation" and "The Crow". Thus, Ezekiel rejoices the themes of degradation of woman, love and sex, and practices of blind beliefs in his poetry in order to depict Indian ethos and culture.

The Unfinished Man is a volume of poems written in the transitory period of personal questioning and moral values exposing peculiar ethos:

> Ezekiel was brought up in an age of great causes where all was to be sacrificed for the big idea. He aspired to make everything subservient to his need to be a poet. The writing of poetry was more than just ambition and vocation; it was a crusade, to be forging a new tradition, evolving a new idiom appropriate to the spirit of a free, secular, more self-reflective modern India. (Anklesaria xxvi)

Mostly, the volume has impact of Ezekiel's association with the city of Bombay which seeks relevance only to modern India. The volume also ensures Ezekiel's self-appraisal to urban ethos. Modern urban life has become the major theme of Ezekiel's poetry reflecting Indian ethos and culture. Despite the ugliness, din, squalor and wickedness of a city like Bombay, Ezekiel has deep affection for the city. He tries to expose its beauty, grandeur, and grace. He attempts to visit whole India through the city of Bombay with its problems concerning poverty, attitude and real life of its people. The theme of urban life finds a proper place in all the anthologies published by Ezekiel. In short "Contemporary India is among the major theme of Ezekiel's poetry", the other being, according to poet himself, "love, personal integration, modern urban life, and spiritual values" (Daruwalla, "Two Decades of Indian Poetry 1960–1980" 56).

In fact, these themes are obvious in Ezekiel's lyrics like, "Urban," "Portrait," "A Morning Walk," "Enterprise," "Case

Study," "Love Sonnet," "Event," "Marriage" and "Virginal". Therefore, the city of Bombay has become central to Ezekiel's poetic thought and an integral part of his poetics. Such a city has a harmful influence on Indian ethos and culture.

However, *The Exact Name* records the confirmation of his root in India. "Despite being city-bred and urban in sensibility, the poet tried to reach out to the centre-stage of cultural ethos in poems like "Night of the Scorpion", "Island" and "In India" (S. Mishra 118). He takes risk of representing reality of Indian society and consequently its ethos and culture:

> Now that he had 'found his roots' he wishes to look for 'the exact name' *i.e.,* 'the right idiom' to avoid all chances of misrepresenting reality. The poems included in this volume were written during 1960-64. They demonstrate his absorption in the indigenous scenario marked by a keen and penetrating observation with no tinge of any inhibitions. He freely looks at the Indian cultural ethos in all its multiplicity and diversity. (S. Mishra 84)

In fact, the chapter shows its need to scrutinize and analyze the early phase of Ezekiel's poetry in order to deal separately in terms of reflection of Indian ethos and culture to achieve special significance to the present study. It is seen that in this phase while presenting Indian ethos and culture, Ezekiel has dealt with the romantic mood and the realistic portrait of Indian societal practices. Thus, the present chapter shows its appropriateness in this study.

Works Cited

Abidi, S.Z.H. *Studies in Indo Anglian Poetry.* Bareilly: Prakash Book Depot, 1978, 293. Print.

Anklesaria, Havovi, Ed. "A Fragment found among Nissim Ezekiel's papers". *Nissim Ezekiel Remembered.* New Delhi: Sahitya Akademi, 2008, 393. Print.

________, Ed. "Interview with Imtiaz and Anil Dharker". *Nissim Ezekiel Remembered.* New Delhi: Sahitya Akademi, 2008, xxvi-44. Print.

Chindhade, Shirish. *Five Indian English Poets.* New Delhi: Atlantic Publishers and Distributors, 2009, 31. Print.

Daruwalla, Keki N. *Collected Poems 1970-2005.* New Delhi: Penguin Books, 2006, 193. Print.

________, Ed. *Two Decades of Indian Poetry 1960–1980,* New Delhi: Vikas, 1980, 56. Print.

Das, Bijay Kumar. *The Horizon of Nissim Ezekiel's Poetry.* New Delhi: B.K. Publishing Corporation, 1995, 7. Print.

________. "Imagery in the Poetry of Nissim Ezekiel." *Perspectives on Nissim Ezekiel.* Ed. S.C. Dwivedi. New Delhi: Kitab Mahal, 1989, 12-19. Print.

Das, Kamala. *Summer in Calcutta.* New Delhi: Everest Press, 1965, 39. Text.

Dwivedi, A.N. *Kamala Das and Her Poetry.* New Delhi: Atlantic Publishers and Distributors, 2011, 22-26. Print.

Ezekiel, Nissim. *Collected Poems.* New Delhi: O.U.P., 2005. Text. All subsequent references to Ezekiel's poems shall be from this edition.

________. "What is Indian in Indo-English Poetry." *Critical Responses: Common-Wealth Literature.* Ed. Dept. of English Osmania U., New Delhi: Sterling P., 38. Print.

Hess, Linda. *Post-Independence Indian Poetry in English,* Spring 49 (1966): 30. Print.

Joshi, Prakash. "Attitudinal Dichotomy in Nissim Ezekiel's Poetry". *Perspectives on Nissim Ezekiel.* Ed. S.C. Dwivedi. New Delhi: Kitab Mahal, 1989, 251. Print.

King, Bruce. *Modern Indian Poetry in English.* Delhi: OUP, 1987, 98. Print.

Kumar, Satish. *A Survey of Indian English Poetry.* Bareilly: Prakash Book Depot, 2001, 178. Print.

Mahan, Shaila. *The Poetry of Nissim Ezekiel.* Jaipur: Classic P., 2001, 8. Print.

Mishra, Sanjit. *The Poetic Art of Nissim Ezekiel.* New Delhi: Atlantic Publishers and Distributors, 2001, 50-118. Print.

Naik, M.K. "The Indianness of Indian Poetry in English." *Indian Poetry in English.* ed. H.M. Prasad. Aurangabad: Parimal P., 1983, 33. Print.

________. "The Tale is in the Sting." *Dimension of Indian English Literature*. New Delhi: Sterling, 1984, 39-40. Print.

Patil, J. Birje. "Interior Cadences: The Poetry of Nissim Ezekiel." *The Literary Criterion*. 2-3.12. ed. C.D. Narasimhaiah. (1976): 209. Print.

Patil, Suresh Pandurang. "Nissim Ezekiel: A Poet of Social Conscience." *Galaxy: International Multidisciplinary Research Journal* 2.1 (April 2012): 1-3. Print.

Ramanujan, A.K. *Collected Poems*. Delhi: OUP, 1997, 38. Text.

Saha, S.C. "Nissim Ezekiel's Contribution to Indian English Poetry". *Contemporary Indian Literature in English: A Humanistic Perspective*. ed. Mithilesh K. Pandey, New Delhi: Kalyani P., 1999, 93. Print.

Shahane, V.A. "The Religious Philosophical Strain in Nissim Ezekiel's Poetry." *Perspective on Nissim Ezekiel*. Ed. S.C. Dwivedi. Allahabad: K.M. Agencies 1989, 22. Print.

Thakur, Guruprasad. "Reflection on Ezekiel's *Night of the Scorpion*". *Perspectives on Nissim Ezekiel*. Ed. S.C. Dwivedi. New Delhi: Kitab Mahal, 1989, 74. Print.

Verma, K.D. "Myth and Imagery in The Unfinished Man: A Critical Reading." *Journals of South Asian Literature*. 11.3-4 (Spring-Summer, 1976): 231. Print.

Wesly, John, and Chandra, N.D.R. "Cultural Complexity in Nissim Ezekiel's Works". *The Criterion: An International Journal in English* 3.3 (September 2012): 9. Print.

5 Indian Ethos and Culture in Nissim Ezekiel's Poetry—II

This chapter studies the reflection of Indian ethos and culture in Ezekiel's recent verse—*Poster Poems* (1969), *Hymns in Darkness* (1976), *Latter-Day Psalms* (1982), and the Latest Poems in *Collected Poems* (1989). The earlier ironic bite and satirical exposure acquire a milder tone and sympathetic colour in this phase. Religio-philosophic strain is one of the characteristics of Ezekiel's recent verse—*Poster Poems*, *Hymns in Darkness* and *Latter-Day Psalms* as it reflects a shift in attitude. His earlier verse is marked with this strand to some extent. On the other hand, Ezekiel tries to bring it with a new form and significance in his recent verse. Actually, he was not a follower of any particular religion or thought of religion. But he was a man of God and his religion was a religion of love, affection, ideals, and charity.

In this phase, Ezekiel seems to be a mature exponent of humanity as his recent poetry reflects his grand level of thought towards societal aspects. Therefore, here the reflection of Indian ethos and culture aspire a genuine importance than in the earlier chapter. Sanjit Mishra puts:

> With the growing age, the poet assumes the role of a grand old man impelled by an urge to bless humanity and in that one can visualize the sublimation of the early Ezekiel ambition to achieve "a human balance humanly" in preference to "the perfect charity of saints" and "the tyrant's endless power" (*CP* 40). The relentless pursuit of objectification and an impelling drive to come out of

> the self acquire a dimension as never before, a magnitude of concern which betrays the typical Indian trait of Vasudhaika Kutumbakam (The whole world as family). The poetic graph since the publication of Hymns in Darkness typically demonstrates the spiritual ambience almost overshadowing other commitments. (120)

In his early phase, Ezekiel seems to be the poet of body and carnal desires to a little extent while his recent phase reveals his maturity in thoughts:

> Ezekiel as a poet has in recent years shown a greater command over his art, a deeper maturity in thought, a more delicate sense of craft, a higher sensitive awareness of words and their poetical content, a more skillful tightness in organization and a deeper inward awareness of the organic form of a poem than in the past. These qualities of the latter phase of Nissim Ezekiel's poetry are relevant to the religious and philosophical poems which are my main topic. (Shahane, "Perspective on Nissim Ezekiel" 22)

An honest effort has been made in this chapter to survey Ezekiel's poems chronologically in order to trace his development as a poet of Indian ethos and culture. While analyzing his poetry, only select poems have been discussed. The emphasis is on Ezekiel's rootedness in the place and trying to come in terms with the ethos and culture of India. His poem "Background, Casually" expresses appropriately Ezekiel's root and heritage. Though published in 1965, this poem remained uncollected until the publication of his next volume *Hymns in Darkness* (1976). This piece inserted in a group of poems (1965-1974) written in between *The Exact Name* and *Hymns* in the *Collected Poems*. Therefore, the poem must be analyzed along with these poems.

In "Background, Casually," the poet ironically expresses his problem of alienation and human relationship. Thus, irony in Ezekiel's poetry is born out of self-consciousness and distrust for easy solutions and readymade formulas. In this respect Ezekiel is a modern Indian English poet. As in the same poem, the poet ironically assesses his lack of strong religious or regional identity. Indian irony is innocent, simple and sensitive. While speaking about Indian irony Mokashi-Punekar rightly remarks, "The Indian irony is less intellectual, more emotive, simple and tragic: The bride is sent to her father-in-law's place!" (18).

Nissim Ezekiel traces the ordinary events of the common man bringing out the weakness of Indian society through the treatment of irony. In "Background, Casually," Ezekiel has treated the caste-bound attitude of the Christians, the Muslims and the Hindus. The poet describes his bitter experience at Roman Catholic school. He was ill treated at the hands of the Christian boys because he was a Jew and his people crucified Christ. This is the caste-bound attitude of Christian community. He was equally ill treated by the Muslims and the Hindus. The poet expresses his ethos:

> I went to Roman Catholic school,
> A mugging Jew among the wolves.
> They told me I had killed the Christ,
> That year I won scripture prize.
> A Muslim sportsman boxed my ears. (*CP* 179)

In short, the poet proves his superiority over Christian by winning a trophy in a scripture contest.

An attempt has been made to show the greatness of Ezekiel in bringing out the ethos and culture of the Christian, the Muslims, and the Hindus in just two stanzas. How easily and sharply has he presented the reality in Indian society concerning the caste-bound attitude of the three communities? May be he wants to touch the sensitive subject "diversity in unity". Thus, he succeeds in his motive.

The poet feels himself as a helpless victim of religious discrimination as expressed in the poem:

> I grew in terror of the strong
> But undernourished Hindu lads,

Their prepositions always wrong,
Repelled me by passivity.
One noisy day I used a knife. (*CP* 179)

Ezekiel also deals with the ethos and culture of the Hindu community. They are undernourished, but they are strong by only from their overwhelming majority in India, and they can terrorize the poor Jew. The poet tries to hate them, as their prepositions are always wrong, they are dullards, inactive and lazy. The poet has to use his knife to defend himself from such Hindu lads. There is a continuous feeling of contempt about Hindus in the poem. He expresses:

How to feel it home, was the point.
Some reading had been done, but what
Had I observed, except my own
Exasperation? All Hindus are
Like that, my father used
  to say,
When someone talked too loudly, or
Knocked at the door like the devil.
They hawked and spat. They sprawled around. (*CP* 180)

It becomes difficult for Ezekiel to feel at home even in the place of his birth due to the spiritual conflicts between two cultures. It is his prejudice that Hindus are known for their roughness and unsophisticated ways. It seems that he has problem of adjusting himself to his place. He faced confusion regarding feeling at home. Despite these circumstances, he decided to live in India and accept the country of his choice.

Ezekiel's childhood memories are also recollected in the poem. It really reminds him of his past in the lines:

The song of my experience sung
I knew that all was yet to sing
My ancestors among the castes
Were aliens crushing seed for breed
(The hooded bullock made his rounds) (*CP* 180)

It comes to know that his ancestors belong to the Saturday oil pressing caste known as *Shanwar Tallies* (Indian caste). Thus, he highlights the caste system of India and the response of Indians to it.

In the same poem, he remembers the hooded bullock which goes round and round crushing the seeds. It continues moving round the machine and never sees around it. It is destined to do the same task for the whole life. This may be symbolic of inaction in life. Thus, the poet's inaction to decide his home country can be seen. Ultimately, Ezekiel comes to resolution; "The Indian landscape sears my eyes / I have become a part of it / to be observed by foreigners" (*CP* 181). In short, in the poem "Background, Casually":

> The opening stanza of the third and final section dwells on the contribution of Ezekiel's to the cultural and the historical life of the Indian nation. Adopting a rather defensive posture, the poet regrets that his family of oil crushers could not add substantially to the native ethos, the only exception in social, literary, and political terms was one of his ancestors his paternal grandfather Haskelji Israel who had fought in the Boer War of 1880s on the British behalf. Even this claim of having shared a racial past has its own pangs of conscience because it was somebody else's war fought wearing British arms, and to that extent a mercenary enterprise. That the racial history cannot absolve him of a reprehensible conscience compelled him to go in for other options by way of ensuring his active involvement in environment. (S. Mishra 99)

Ezekiel's most remarkable poem "Transparently" appeared in the group of poems composed during 1965-1974. The poem reveals the note of confusion and despair and also highlights the poet's transparent sincerity to accept the truth of life:

> All I want now
> is the recognition
> of dilemma

and the quickest means
of resolving it
within my limits. (*CP* 150)

In his poem "In the Theatre," Ezekiel tries to know the cosmic power of intelligence and the God's truth to feel metaphysical transcendentalism:

I act to end the acting,
not to be known but to know,
to be new, to become a form and find
my relevance. (*CP* 151)

Ezekiel wonders in the dilemma—"to be or not to be" and faces the evils to confirm the place of his choice. It happens naturally without any force of circumstances. In his poem "After Reading a Prediction", he confesses:

This is the place
where I was born, I
know it
well. It is home,
which I recognize at last
as a kind of hell
to be made tolerable. (*CP* 155)

It reminds A.K. Ramanujan's poem "Conventions of Despair" where the poet is not ready to exchange his 'hell' with someone's heaven. He says, "I must seek and will find / my particular hell only in my hindu mind" (Ramanujan 34). Ezekiel finds so weary with the concept of heaven that he doesn't mind to appreciate hell. He says that "There is one thing to be said for hell / It's pretty lively place / a man could be happy there" (*CP* 220).

Ezekiel's attachment to the place of his choice is permanent. His emotional philosophy of humanism is different. He seeks closeness with people of India and consequently their ethos and culture. It is seen in his poem "Happening":

The food I eat
cannot nourish me
unless I love the human face
I close the door and sit alone
in kinship with the word. (*CP* 164)

In *Hymns in Darkness*, the darkness symbolizes of the fall in spiritual and cultural values. The volume continuously presents the degradation of religious, political, social and spiritual values. The poet, in his *Hymns in Darkness*, is seen praying God for demanding positive strength with purpose to get rid of this degradation of values in Indian society. Ezekiel's contemporary novelist Naipaul also wrote travelogue "An Area of Darkness".

> It is not a mere coincidence that 'darkness' occurs as a principal term both in Naipaul's controversial travelogue "An Area of Darkness". By darkness the celebrated novelist means the external unhealthy manifestations like illiteracy and ignorance that characterized his ancestors' country during his visit in the early sixties. His vision was confined simply to the surface realities and could not penetrate the deeper connotation of 'darkness' which is central to the Indian spiritual experience—*Tamaso ma jyotirgamaya* (lead me from darkness to light). In Ezekiel's poem it literary means the darkness of the fallen spirit in contrast to those who live by spiritual illumination. Negatively it may mean a mystic way or state of salvation—the Divine can be unknowable darkness as well as light. (S. Mishra 115)

However, *Hymns in Darkness* is a collection of sixteen sections which are displayed scattered in his early poetry. Ezekiel's spiritual attitude has prevailed throughout the volume. At the same time, Ezekiel's love for the depiction of a pagan woman is not disassociated from his recent poetry.

The most embracing fact of Ezekiel's poetry written in his last phase is his description of woman's seductive attitude.

In *Hymns in Darkness* the seductive attitude of woman is highlighted in "Three Women", "Motives", "In Twenty Four Hours" and "Haiku". The woman pretends not to make a sex play, yet 'connives all the same' to force the man to sexual union. In "Motives", the man's frank attitude of considering woman as a sex object is also reflected:

> My motives are sexual,
> aesthetic and friendly
> in that order, adding up
> to have with you. (*CP* 154)

As he comes close to woman, her anatomy, majestic and charming, casts a magic spell on him and he says: "Yours thighs are full and round / thin and flat I'd love them too / There go my aesthetics" (*CP* 154). In "Haiku" the woman blatantly—"brought out her small / breasts, to be caressed" (*CP* 174). Ezekiel's quest for identity makes him a minute observer of Indian society as well its persona and institutions which lack normal humanity. It helps him to be satirical in tone. As a result of it, his poem "Three Women" is a satire on morally loose women who offer people not only food but also love and the poet says:

> They spoke the language
> of food and love
> naturally
> as a mother-tongue
> no problem here
> or accent or of intonation. (*CP* 151)

In *Latter-Day Psalms* woman's seductive attitude is captured in "Nudes II 1978":

> This one announces every act
> of pleasure as she does it.
> 'I love undressing', she has to say,
> as she undresses. The verbal
> and the visual join in her.

'Is this a part of you?' she asks,
as she holds it, stares at it.
Then she laughs. 'Put your finger
There,' she pleads, as if
I need instructions. It's only
impatience, though, becoming frenzy
as I penetrate. 'Now,' she claims,
you are within me. 'Aren't you
within me?' And she makes me say, 'I am'. (*CP* 246)

In this poem, the poet paints the nude woman from the eye of an artist. He tries to come with her nude beauty from the point of view of art and painting. This realization makes to understand life. In this manner, Bruce King comments:

> The naked is scientific, the nude is cultured. We see the world with a naked eye. People are nudist not nakedists. Ezekiel uses this distinction both to examine the social arts that accompany seduction and to draw a parallel between his poems and a painter's series of nude portraits in which format qualities and matter are of equal interest. Thus, the poems shift rapidly between discussion of the women as forms, as art, as objects of desire, as individuals, and there is a constant secondary significance, as discussion of form and experience can also refer to the art of poetry. (48)

However, many Indian English Poets try to depict woman as a sex instrument in the modern society. Jayant Mahapatra also tries to bring the reality about a woman. He, therefore, expresses the height of degradation of human morality in his poem "Hunger". A fisherman who is poor, doesn't hesitate to sale the flesh of his fifteen years old daughter. The poet emphasizes that the poverty compels man to sell the body of his own daughter. It reveals the hunger for both food and carnal desire. It exposes stark reality of our contemporary India society:

> I heard him say; my daughter, she's just turned fifteen...
> feel her. I'll be back soon, your bus leaves at nine.
> the sky fell on me, and a father's exhausted wile.
> long and lean, her years were cold as rubber.
> she opened her wormy legs wide. Felt the hunger there,
> the other one, the fish slithering, turning inside. (Mahapatra 46)

Again, the image of pagan woman appears in Ezekiel's poetry. On the other hand, one noticeable thing in Ezekiel's poetry is that male persona's attitude does not treat woman on equal level. He does not think that woman has a mind for sexual fulfillment along with flesh and blood:

> A close study of the essence of the male persona's attitude in such relationships as presented in these poems gives the impression that the male persona's aim in these encounters is not fulfillment or consummation of love but an indifferent observation to analyze, testify and prove or disprove some point. (Kurup 88)

Thus, in his recent poetry "The tone of indifference and empathy in attitude is evident" (Kurup 88).

The attitude of Indian parents to absorb all pain and wish all sorts of troubles off from their children's life signifies the sense of Indianness. In "For Kalpana," the poet and his wife take seriously the illness of their daughter. The seriousness is obvious in the lines:

> And they watch their child daily
> eating breakfast
> greasy egg-yolk egg-white
> jams, jellies, toast and porridge
> fat with the milk of human kindness
> or dinner
> of curry-drowned rice
> and momentous salad

eat eat my child
how thin you are. (qtd. in Karnani 142)

The seriousness of looking after the daughter reflects the parents' genuine affectionate and lovable attitude. Despite their efforts when nothing happens, they develop a kind of jealous attitude towards other people's children. This common thread of Indian ethos and culture is revealed in the lines:

so the child looks down
distastefully
and eats and eats
but it does no good
while other people's children
grow pink and plump
on fresh air and foolishness. (qtd. in Karnani 143)

Ezekiel's poetry is a living record of Indian values and its changing face. Exploring the man-woman relationship, Ezekiel's tongue does not slip to expose the changing attitude of lover and beloved. It is felt that Ezekiel tries to reveal the change in attitude based on past love experience of people in the real life. He very skillfully handles the theme of love and sex and exposes lover's changing attitude of breaking up the affair. In "Poem of the Separation," Ezekiel describes his sufferings when he has to break up with his beloved. He remembers the meetings with his beloved:

Any man may be a whirlwind,
any woman lightning
but buses take us to our meeting,
trains to our destination.
In these, and in cafes,
on beaches,
and on benches in the park
our music was made. (*CP* 196)

The poet describes modern places where he used to meet his beloved. The places of meetings are changed time to time and so is the depth of love. It is thought that love made in buses, trains, cafes, beaches, benches in the park cannot last forever as these are the symbols of temporary life. Hence, such love can easily shatter to pieces. On the other hand, the attitude to understand and accept beloved's reason for wanting to break up the affair is expressed in the last stanza of the poem:

> But you ask to break it up.
> Your latest letter says:
> "I am enclosing
> Ramanujan's translation
> of a Kannada religious poem:
> 'The Lord is playing
> With streamers of fire.'
> I want to play with fire...
> Let me get burnt". (*CP* 196)

The poem "The Couple" is one of Ezekiel's many love poems. It appeals that love can be genuine, emotional, spiritual and physical. Ezekiel believes in physical love of sex. Man always expects to get full satisfaction from woman. Therefore, he praises her and makes her feel that she is beautiful. He calls her a wonderful woman and she exposes her body to full co-operation:

> She did it pretty enough,
> demonstrating
> with childlike glee
> a trick or two. (*CP* 183)

Indeed, the poet goes deep into the hearts of Indians either they are lovers or ordinary persons. Thus, woman is flexible to co-operate at any condition. While speaking about love and sex, Shiv K. Kumar's poetry seems to be arresting for its different thoughts. He thinks that love and sex are one and essential in maintaining the relationship between man and woman. In his poem, Shiv K. Kumar says:

Even in bed
myself
Copulates with its own dry bones
leaving her body
pensile on the tide's crest. (qtd. in Satish Kumar 218)

In Shiv K. Kumar's poetry, love and sex are intuitive as Satish Kumar points out:

> Love, sex and marriage occupy an important place in Kumar's poetry. He glorifies intuitive love and the natural satiation of sexual urge. Love is self-surrender. It is beyond logical comprehension and intellectual discussion. Falling in love at first sight is not based on logical reasoning; it is purely intuitive, involuntary response to life. Love and sex are one. Sex is a form of intuitive energy which needs instantaneous outlet. To Kumar sex is the basis of all emotional relationship between man and woman, and it, therefore, should not be condemned as ugly or indecent. Sex stands for openness, acceptance and self-surrender. In the course of the act of love or in the moment of sexual union there are no spoken words, no verbalization, no discussion. He discards the intuition of marriage because it hinders the free flow of love. (218)

Ezekiel equally explores the present ethos and culture of Indian *Sadhus* in his poetry. India is a land of saint's tradition, a token of spirituality, morality and humanity. But the word 'saint' has lost its meaning today and Ezekiel as a true Indian poet satires the hypocritical attitude of the saints and the slavish Indian attitude of the people who become the victim of the hypocrisy. Ezekiel portrays the reality in his poem "Guru":

But then we learn
the saint is still a faithless friend,
obstinate in argument,
ungrateful for favours done
hard with servants and the poor,

> discourteous to disciples, especially men,
> condescending, even rude
> to visitor (except the foreigners)
> and over scrupulous in checking
> the account of the ashram.
> He is also fat. (*CP* 192)

Here Ezekiel deals with the religious hypocritical attitude of the Indian *sadhus*. Bringing forth the hypocrisy, Ezekiel says that these saints are the false *gurus* who only make religious exhibition and deceive the servants and the poor. They have become fat by eating the food of the *ashram*. They have made religion commercial by checking the accounts of the *ashram*. Such saints never grow the hopes of the people but lead them to pessimistic attitude:

> Fake god-men are a curse to India. The guru in the poem possesses all the vices that a saint or guru must never be guilty of: he is faithful, obstinate, ungrateful, merciless to servants and the poor, discourteous to disciples, rude to visitors (except the foreigners), money-minded, unrestrained in fleshy enjoyments, and what not?—almost a walking museum of vices. After this exhaustive cataloguing of the guru's vices, the poem butts into a very direct, prosy, rhetorical conclusion. (Chindhade 46-47)

In this connection, Keki N. Daruwalla's poem "Vignette-II" also pictures ironically the rituals and sacred rites performed on the banks of river, Ganga. Here, the poet tries to bring out the attitude of Indian *Sadhu's* guiding on the *ghat*:

> Women do not take off their saris
> as they enter the water;
> men leave their clothes behind.
> The dead leave their bodies. (Daruwalla 102)

In the above lines, the poet's tone is of a sarcastic one. He ridiculously puts the situation with a bizarre status. He says, "A blind man's fingers gripe across my face / A sadhu eyes me unblinking from his navel" (Daruwalla 102).

Ezekiel says, "If saints are like this / what hope is there then for us" (*CP* 192). The people come to the so-called *Gurus* to seek holy advice, and peace of mind. But these cheats are discourteous to male disciples. This proves that they are lustful in characters. As Rajendra Nath Mishra says, "They are not above mundane wants as they show secret inclination towards lady disciples. What could be more hopeless than this attitude of these saints?" (12).

The poem "Guru" seems to be written with the aim to reflect Indian ethos and culture. Ezekiel appeals the corrupt attitude and finds a reform: "As the champion of social reformation, his intense humanism is the defense disguised in a social cry. The wide range of his poems on social problems denotes his genuine urge for social upliftment of the poor, a sincere effort to demolish the wide gap between the two poles of Indian society" (Patil 4).

Perhaps Ramanujan has a similar view on the nature of Indian *gurus* as he satirically points out in his poem "The Guru":

> Forgive the weasel his tooth
> forgive the tiger his claw
> But do not forgive the woman
> her malice or the man his envy
> Said the guru
> Give the dog his bone, the parrot
> his seed, the pet snake his mouse
> But do not give woman her freedom
> nor man his midday meal till he begs
> Said the guru. (Ramanujan 251)

Another catching feature of Ezekiel's poetry is his use of *Babu Angrezi*. Scarcely any poet among the Post-Independence poets like Nissim Ezekiel has depicted the cultural ethos of Indians by employing *Swadeshi Angrezi*. On the other hand, he has also made fun of craze for foreign things as seen in his poem

"Goodbye Party for Miss Pushpa T.S." The poem has a touch of social satire wherein he tries to expose the follies of Indian *Sahib* and *Memsahib* in using incorrect English and the foreign habits.

The poet very artistically evokes a farewell speech to bid goodbye to Miss Pushpa T. S. He describes internal as well as external beauty of Miss Pushpa in *Babu Angrezi*. He says:

> You are all knowing, friends,
> what sweetness is in Miss Pushpa.
> I don't mean only external sweetness
> but internal sweetness.
> Miss Pushpa is smiling and smiling
> even for no reason
> but simply because she is feeling. (*CP* 190)

The lines, on the other hand, remind us of William Shakespeare's famous line from *Hamlet* "One may smile and smile and be a villain". In spite of Ezekiel's intention to depict Miss Pushpa as a flirt, the poet at the same time asserts the positive reason of her smile and builds a living example of Indian ethos and culture.

Ezekiel makes a digression in the same poem from the main concern. He employs the idea which is not related to the main theme of the poem. This is another striking typical Indian way of thinking and speaking English. The poet speaks of himself and makes a digression, which is obvious in the lines:

> I am not remembering now which place.
> Surat? Ah, yes,
> once only I stayed in Surat
> with family members
> of my uncle's very old friend–
> his wife was cooking nicely...
> that was long time ago. (*CP* 190)

The digression is entirely unconnected with the main concern of the poem. It seems that the speech is rambling and even the logical connectives between ideas are missing. But typical is the Indian way of thinking and speaking.

After the digression, the poet continues to describe various good things in the behavior of Miss Pushpa. At the same time, he expresses the ethos and culture of Indian ladies of always responding in positive. The poet says:

> Pushpa Miss is never saying no.
> Whatever I or anybody is asking
> she is always saying yes,
> and today she is going
> to improve her prospects
> and we are wishing her bon voyage. (*CP* 191)

The poet expresses that Miss Pushpa is always eager to help anybody at anytime. It is her attitude not to say 'no'. He praises her good nature. He has treated ironically the affections and pretensions. He satirically comments on the mental vacuity of Indian girls and ladies. "Typically Indian in its laxity and shallowness the entire poem is a biting satirical comment on the way we speak and respond to various situations. In his simplistic ignorance the fellow hardly knows whether he is complimentary or critical to poor Miss Pushpa" (Chindhade 41).

One cannot avoid noticing the humour in most of Ezekiel's poetry used as a weapon of satire. His *Very Indian Poems in Indian English* are characterized by ease, irony, wit and humour. In his other poems, Ezekiel also deals with the humour, but in these poems, he imparts typical Indian flavour to English language. In these poems, as a critic of society, Ezekiel mocks some Indians and their way of using English.

Another important feature of the poem is the use of capital letters for the first words of each line. Thus, the poet introduces some technical innovation. The language is colloquial and so are the rhythms. Instead of conventional versification, the poet has used free verse or verse libre.

Indeed, Ezekiel has the potential to create a sense of Indianness by employing *Babu Angrezi*. Perhaps Ezekiel attempts to turn language into an artifact as it has a cold, glass-like quality and he succeeds. After Furtado, Ezekiel is the only poet to have seriously considered the use of pidgin English, notably in poems like "A Very Indian Poem in Indian English," "Goodbye Party for Miss Pushpa T.S." and "The Professor" (Parthasarathy 8). Therefore, it is not an exaggeration to say that Ezekiel excels among the Post-Independence poets in his use of *Babu Angrezi* or *Bazaar English* to depict the characteristic Indian attitude. In fact, he enjoys more freedom in describing the Indian ethos and culture than his contemporaries.

In his poem "How the English Lessons Ended", the poet describes the Indian psyche and the native scenario. Generally, in Muslim community, the females are not allowed to take education. On the other side, Ezekiel shows the changing attitude of Muslim community and consequently their acceptance of Indian culture. In the poem "How the English Lessons Ended", the parents in Muslim family want their daughter to be tutored in English. It is a different matter that the girl instead of studying is seen indulged in enjoying obscene pictures during the tuition hours. The morally conscious parent stops the tuition and the girl is married off. The poet says:

> They probably decide I made advances,
> and almost hint as much
> to my poor mother, who's outraged.
> There is gratitude for you, she says,
> That girl will never get a husband! (*CP* 201)

The Indians have a tradition of not telling directly, particularly to the male head of the family. The poet expresses it in the same poem: "My daughter tells my wife / who tells my mother / who tells me. I laugh it off" (*CP* 201).

In course of his treatment of ordinary life, Ezekiel highlights underlying Indian ethos and culture which is rooted in fatalism. Indians try to achieve success without making efforts. This attitude of Indians is clearly captured by Ezekiel in his poem "The Railway Clerk". The poem exposes pathetic condition of the railway clerk. He symbolizes the helplessness of poor Indians who anticipate too much without hard work. The poet says:

> My wife is always asking for more money,
> Money, money, where to get money?
> My job is such, no one is giving bribe,
> while other clerks are in fortunate position... (*CP* 184)

The protagonist is a victim of official bossism and unable to meet the simple demands of his wife due to low salary. The all-pervading corruption in the "Indian Clerical Services" is also hit on here. Ezekiel seems to be the critic of societal practices. "His sympathetic approach carries him very close to the legacy of social reformer disguised as a poet" (Patil 1). The poem not only echoes the social condition but also shows the comical use of English. The poem falls in the category of *Very Indian Poems in Indian English*. The protagonist wins our sympathy by using faulty English:

> I am never neglected my responsibility,
> I am discharging it properly,
> I am doing my duty.
> but who is appreciating?
> Nobody, I am telling you. (*CP* 184)

Another poem "Yashwant Jagtap" also exposes the ethos and culture of the poor Indians rooted in fatalism. The poem is a haunting description of a poor man affected by flood. He places the child on the shoulder when the water rises high. The same situation reminds of the Mahabharata, the great epic poem of Hinduism, when Kansa wanted to kill the little Krishna, Vasudev, the father of Krishna, saved the life of his son by carrying him on his head to the safe place when water rose high in the river. The pathetic condition of a poor man is also expressed in the poem:

He is sixty, the child eleven,
He pushes a handcart–
earn a rupee a day.
A true-blue Indian he
is reconciled to his lot,
and so are we. (qtd. in Nandy 9)

In his poem "The Truth about the Floods," Ezekiel exposes the apathetic and indifferent attitudes of the Government officials who are only in collecting "statistics of the relief work". This corrupt attitude of Indians finds its root in injustice or low salary. However, the poem also throws light on the lack of education and source of entertainment, which results in the long line of children mostly in poor class. The situation definitely highlights the illiteracy and the consequences of overpopulation. The poet satirizes here:

A villager speaks:
I have eleven children.
Two I have left to the mercy of God.
The rest are begging, somewhere. (*CP* 186)

Ezekiel voices against the rampant poverty which seems to be the main reason of many social ills. The same poem gives the grim picture of poverty. The flood affected victims of Bihar are captured in his poem:

The villagers ran to them.
They slapped their bellies
and whined:
'I have not eaten for three days.'
'My husband has been washed away.'
'My parents have abandoned me.'
'My son is dying.'
'I cannot find my daughter.' (*CP* 187)

Another tendency of exploitation of the weaker by the stronger is marked today in Indian society:

> It may not be all correct but what the poet emphasizes is the truth that most of the people involved in the relief and rescue work perform duties sans love and mercy. A simple narration evokes pathos and that is its strength. Nissim Ezekiel speaks about the destruction floods bring to villagers and people and make even the local officials helpless in rendering adequate assistance. Here he underlines the unsympathetic attitude of the people supposed to provide relief. (Prem 117)

Ramanujan also describes the same pathos of flood affected people. He gives horrible picture of a house, a pregnant woman and cow which wash away in flood in his poem "A River":

> He said:
> the river has water enough
> to be poetic
> about only once a year
> and then
> it carries away
> in the first half hour
> three village houses,
> a couple of cows
> named Gopi and Brinda.
> and one pregnant woman. (Ramanujan 38)

Keki N. Daruwalla in his poem "The Ghaghra in Spate" equally depicts a murderous river when overflows. It washes and destroys everything that comes in the way. It is a symbol of destruction. The poet describes the scene:

> And suddenly at night
> the north comes to the village
> riding on river-back
> Twenty minutes of a nightmare spin
> and fear turns phantasmal

as half a street goes
churning in the river belly. (Daruwalla 74-75)

Nissim Ezekiel, in his poem "Rural Suite," brings out the ethos and culture of Indians:

It's a shameless exploitation
of people's ignorance.
It's not even as if they need the food:
most of them are wealthy farmers
from the neighbouring village
with a taste for hoarding, gold. (*CP* 197)

Ezekiel makes fun of the cheap restaurants in Bombay in his poem "Irani Restaurant Instructions" and brings the ethos and culture of Indians. In Bombay, the cheap restaurants display bizarre boards as:

Do not write letter
Without order refreshment
Do not comb,
Hair is spoiling floor
Do not make mischiefs in cabin
our water is reporting. (*CP* 240)

Here lies the greatness of Ezekiel to mock the cheapness of the Indian restaurants with the ting of biting irony. Many critics agree that the good combination of subtle irony and subdued humour adequately conceal the arrogance in his poetry. As it is obvious in a poem like "Cows":

She knows that cows are holy,
Worshiped by the parents
of the children in her school.
Even Gods ought not to clutter up
the pavements—that's her view.
She's not against beliefs, believe
What you like, she says,
but get out of my way. (qtd. in Kurup 101)

Ezekiel focuses each thread of Indian life in his poetry. He is aware of the treatment of woman in his poetry. He frankly depicts the various roles played by an Indian woman. Somewhere in his poetry, she is depicted as affectionate mother, wife, and beloved, but somewhere she plays the part of a seductress. Somewhere she is abolished all her rights and is locked only to home and hearth. Many times, she has become the victim in the midst of male-oriented Indian society. In man-woman relationship, she is shown as an object of entertainment in some of Nissim's poetry. He deals with the issue with an optimistic approach and reveals woman's cultural ethos regarding the various situations in life.

It is easy to find a kind of faithful description of the immediate situation reflecting the Indian ethos and culture in Ezekiel's poetry. However, he is aware of every detail of Indian life and paints it without hesitation. He minutely observes the condition of Indian woman. While speaking about his 'Servant', Ezekiel explores a very common Indian attitude of marrying the daughter in a light age of twelve or fourteen. The ethos and culture of accepting every suffering without protest of Indian wife is revealed. These poor servants are ill-treated by their husbands. There is an interesting family situation where the poet's mother tells the ethos of these female servants. Here woman is shown conscious of one thing only:

> At twelve or fourteen, married off
> To the usual brute,
> She has a child,
> and tells my mother every time
> her husband beats her
> for the fun of it.
> weal on the back and thighs. (qtd. in Karnani 161)

But she complains before her mistress instead before her husband. Thus, it is a picture of typically suppressed Indian wife:

> That is a fate of a suppressed Indian wife. In addition to hint at the dirty practices of child-marriage, the poet also tries to comment on man and his destiny. The tormented wife is quite used to it as she thinks it to be quite inevitable in her fate. There is no way out. The poet can observe it as a distance. Nothing can be done as it is one of the several cases of misfortune. (R. Mishra 11)

Again, Ezekiel throws light on the cultural ethos of maid-servants in his poem "Ganga". The poet voices against the treatment given to them by their part-time mistresses. He says:

> She always gets
> a cup of tea
> preserved for her
> from the previous evening,
> and a chapatti, stale
> but in good condition.
> Once a year, an old
> sari and a blouse
> for which we could
> easily exchange a plate
> Or a cup and saucer.
> Besides, she borrows
> Small coins for paan
> or a sweet for her child.
> She brings a smell with her
> and leaves it behind her,
> but we are used to it. (*CP* 202)

The poem brings the characters of both the maid-servant, Ganga and her mistresses. Apart from her wages, Ganga gets extra like a cup of tea, left-over food, old sari, blouse, sweets for her child as a token of her mistresses' generosity. The poem presents everyday fact in Indian society. It brings forth the false generosity of Indians.

The poem "Entertainment" describes a typical Indian scene of monkey show, which exposes the cool ethos and culture of Indians toward animals. The poem describes the pathetic condition of the show master and his monkeys. He cracks whip, drums frenzy and tries all tricks to earn copper coins. Ezekiel brings out the moral in the situation with the help of apt irony and satire:

> The monkey-show is on:
> patient girl on haunches
> holds the strings,
> a baby in her arms.
> Two redy monkeys
> in red and purple pantaloons
> prepare to dance.
> crowd Collects,
> forms a circle..........
> only monkeys are sad,
>
> ....
>
> Anticipating time for payment,
> the crowd dissolves.
> Some, in shame, part
> with the smallest coin they have.
> The show moves on. (*CP* 194)

The poem reflects an authentic Indianness because such roadside shows are very common in any street corner of India. People gather to enjoy the show and fail to pay a single coin. This very meanness of Indian society is captured by the poet. "Entertainment depicts the monkey show, which is a peculiar Indian street scene. The situation is typically Indian. We see the poor Indian society and the meanness of people. They watch the show but do not pay for it and slunk away after the show end" (Mahan 47).

Ezekiel's poem "Island" satirically depicts the standard of living in the city of Bombay. It gives his cultural marginality and a sharp departure from the feeling of alienation for his spiritual past displaces him from his environment. The expansion of city in terms of slums and high rising buildings makes the poet to find his place in it. Living in the midst of people engaged in endless competitions, the poet exposes himself thus: "I hear distorted echoes / of my own ambiguous voice / and of dragons claiming to be human" (*CP* 182). Ezekiel emphasizes not to leave the delightful people's island. He expresses thus:

> How delightful the soul with absolute
> sense of salvation, how
> hold to a single willed direction?
> I cannot leave the island,
> I was born here and belong. (*CP* 182)

He hurries to his daily business as the habit of the island:

> Even now a host of miracles
> hurries me to daily business,
> minding the ways of the island
> as a good native should,
> taking calm and clamour in my stride. (*CP* 182)

The poem reminds Ezekiel's early poem "Urban". There is a long gap of time between the compositions of these two poems. But there seems no distance in Ezekiel's attachment to the city:

> This 'calm and calmour' recalls "kinder clamour close at hand" of "Urban". It is remarkable that even a long gap of thirteen years that elapsed between the compositions of these two poems, Ezekiel's initial attachment to the city remains intact despite its disenchanting features he uninhibitedly exposes. In fact, Ezekiel's poetry inhabits middling ground between a skyscraper and a slum; neither staggering nor hyperbolic, but equally it never fails to overwhelm the reader in its warmth, its humanity and above all its homeliness. (S. Mishra 108-09)

While exploring Indian ethos and culture, Ezekiel drives deep in the psyche of male and female persona. His poem "Song to be Shouted Out" depicts the family problems in India. Where, the wife yells at the husband on coming home in the evening. The husband describes the situation:

I come home in the evening
and my wife shouts at me:
Did you bank that cheque?
Did you buy those tickets?
Did you ask if cheese is in stock or not? (*CP* 241)

He, in typical Indian English, narrates the ethos of the husband troubled by the wife in the poem "Song to be Shouted Out," from *Songs for Nandu Bhende*:

Shout at me, woman!
Pull me up for this and that
You're right and I'm wrong
This is not an excuse,
It's only a song
It's good for my soul
To be shouted at.
Shout at me, woman!
What else are wives for? (*CP* 242)

The incident exposes the true love between husband and wife, though their way of expressing it is different. They fight with each other, but are not ready to live separately. Indian culture could not allow them to take final action. This is the genius of the poet to reflect Indian ethos and culture through small events in human life.

"Poverty Poem" depicts the typical attitudes of the Indian beggars, who capture the innocent foreigners in their trap. While a foreign lady tells the poet how she gave alms to a beggar:

'Before he released me,
he smiled and I smiled back,

I turned and gave him a coin,
past belief in that or anything.' (*CP* 230)

The cunning attitude of Indian beggars is presented in an ironical manner. They know it well that the foreigners are rich and they can give more than the Indians. So they impress by smiling at them:

She didn't know beggars in India
smile only at white, foreigners
'Indians are friendly people, anyway,'
she said. (*CP* 231)

In this connection, Sanjit Mishra observes:

> Ezekiel's dig at the typical trait of Indian beggars who smile only at 'white foreigners' has been frowned upon by many a critic. It has been argued that Ezekiel's non native ancestry surfaces at places in his debunking of Indian phenomena. Reading in between the lines, one feels Ezekiel is articulating his own impressions in that the colour of his skin also resembles the 'white foreigners'. (129)

In Ezekiel's poem "Jewish Wedding in Bombay", the newly married wife invites her husband in candid terms. It takes her ten years to reveal her disappointment. The poem expresses, "More than ten years passed before she told me that / she remembered being very disappointed. Is that all? There is to it? She had wondered" (*CP* 235). However, the Indian wives in Ezekiel's poem are not as modern as they are deserved to be. They never express their inner self that they are not physically satisfied with their husbands. This is the striking candid attitude of Indian wives as exposed by the poet.

In the same poem, the poet describes that the marriage ceremonies are a great part of Indian life. The poet presents the subtleties of the celebration in a typical style. In Indian marriages, there is a tradition of expressing grief by bride and her mother while leaving the house of father. In reality, neither bride nor her mother sheds tears while going to husband's house. This very ethos and culture of Indian bride and her mother is expressed in the lines:

> Her mother shed a tear or two but wasn't really
> crying. It was the thing to do, so she did it,
> enjoying every moment. The bride laughed when I
> sympathized, and said don't be silly. (*CP* 234)

Religio—philosophic strain is another characteristic of Ezekiel's recent verse—*Hymns in Darkness, Latter-Day Psalms*, and *Poster Poems* which reflect a shift in attitude. His earlier verse is marked with this strand to some extent. On the other hand, Ezekiel tries to bring it with a new form and significance in his recent verse. Actually, he was not a follower of any particular religion or thought of religion. But he was a man of God and his religion was a religion of humanity. However, the recent alienation that Ezekiel faces is the religious one, which has become a partial of his poetry. He was a Maharashtrian Jew, but he lacked the knowledge of his mother tongue, Marathi because of his early education in missionary school. As Ezekiel himself says:

> I was brought up in a mildly orthodox Jewish home which gradually became liberal Jewish. I attended the liberal Jewish Synagogue in Bombay until I abandoned religion altogether soon after leaving school. He further claims he does not "get a sense of religion, sustained from day-to-day, in my life. If I write a religious poem, the next poem is likely to be very secular, sceptical. I attach a great deal of importance to the worldliness of the world, its independence. (qtd. in Shahane, *Journal of South Asian Literature* 254)

Ezekiel does not pray God directly, but existence of God cannot escape from his imagination. In his later verse, Ezekiel earns to be religious. He makes it clear: "I am not a religious or even a moral person in any conventional sense. Yet I have always felt myself to be religious and moral in some sense. The gap between these two statements is the existential sphere of my poetry" (qtd. in Shahane 254). Truly, *Latter-Day Psalms* reveals Ezekiel as a religious humanist. "It is surprising how often the word 'prayer' occurs in the work of a poet whose approach to life far from being religious is one of philosophical humanism" (Jussawalla 77).

In his recent age, Ezekiel felt the overwhelming presence of God. It brought about a transforming effect on his consciousness and he began to take interest in Hindu mysticism. Because of it, the religious and mystical tone found expression in his *Hymns in Darkness* and other poems. Besides his social and human concerns, a religious and spiritual touch has become an important factor of his recent poetry. The city dweller, lost in "total darkness," realizes God through self-surrender: "He has lost faith in himself / and found faith at last" (*CP* 219).

Though his poetry reveals religious awareness, Ezekiel hardly acquires the essence of the traditional religious poetry. He combines various traditions of love, philosophy and religion—of Judaism, Hinduism and Christianity. As Michael Garman rightly observes, "He brings to the established traditions of love, religion and the passing hour the modern attitude of the need for a commitment, an existential plunge into life, and of cold analytic disgust, becoming more detached and ironical as he develops" (qtd. in Abidi 291). A survey of his *Hymns in Darkness, Poster Poems* and *Latter-Day Psalms* reveals that the poet "does not consider himself to be alien or an outsider but exercises his will to claim God's love even though he knows that it will not come to him" (qtd. in Tilak 34). Ezekiel wants to meet God to overcome all his worries and problems.

Ezekiel's "The Egoist's Prayers" prevails the echo of Gita where he communicates with God. It was originally titled *Poster Prayers* and exhibited at Gallery Chemould in 1975. In the prayer, the poet speaks to God casually like a friend in an ironic tone. The poem shows the influence of Gita which is a kind of an advice given by Lord Krishna to Arjuna in his hour of inaction whether to kill his cousins. Kauravas in the battlefield. Thus, the poet puts his matter before his God. He feels that God if reminded His duty can rescue the vicious man of his sins:

Kick me around
a bit more, O Lord.
I see at last
there's no other way
for me to learn
your simplest truths.
The vice I've always had
I still have
The virtues I've never had
I still do not have.
From this Human Way of Life
Who can rescue Man
If not his Maker?
Do thy duty, Lord...
Confiscate my passport, Lord,
I do not want to go abroad.
Let me find my song
Where I belong. (*CP* 213)

The poet asks for God's help to suppress his hunger for such worldly pleasures as sex, love and success. He just attempts to find out true and false within himself in order to examine virtue and vice. It clears that the poet wants to discover realities and mysteries of life. In the words of Sataynaraian Singh:

> He is sceptical of deliverance, whether through faith in God's grace or through man's overweening confidence that he is the master of his fate. He underscores the need for humility and sincerity and constant application of the questioning mind. Salvation is a question of neither belief

> nor unbelief. We are all subject to life and mortality. It is given only to earnest and assiduous seekers to discover reality and its mysteries. (qtd. in Tilak 35)

In his opening hymn, the poet presents the quality of humility, the ornament of a self-esteemed person. He makes one to come out his ego and also to make life happy:

> Self-esteem stunts his growth. He has not learnt
> how to be nobody.
> All his truths are outside him,
> and mock his activity. (*CP* 217)

The poet in his second hymn suggests making yogic practices in order to behave like human beings:

> He speaks with his own voice. He listens
> with the Third ear. He sees
> with the eye
> in the centre of his forehead. (*CP* 218)

The line reminds one of the Hindu God *Shiva* who has third eye on his forehead. It is said that the Lord *Shiva* opened his third eye when there were spiritual chaos on the land. The eye has divine power achieved by practicing austerity in Himalaya. In this way, Ezekiel believes in Indian Gods and their teaching of ethos and culture. Ezekiel also asks to leave ego aside in his third prayer.

Ezekiel observes that most of the Indians suffer the relationship for the sake of maintaining relations. This typical mentality of man is presented in his hymns:

> Incapable of quarreling with them
> he maintains the old
> stale
> unredeemable relationships. (*CP* 220)

Ezekiel makes it clear that the secrets of life are concealed by darkness and distorted by light:

> The darkness has its secrets

which light does not know,
It's a kind of perfection,
while every light
distorts the truth. (*CP* 223)

In fact, Ezekiel's hymns have a great influence of Vedas, for they appeal to open the mystery of life based on the pillars of faith and truth. The hymns tell the eternal value and meaning of human life. Thus, this recent phase of poetry expresses exclusive favour and love for humanity. This gives a shocking turn to Ezekiel's recent phase of poetry coming in term of reflection of Indian ethos and culture in his poetry.

In the poem "Hangover" he describes Bombay and therefore changing Indian ethos and culture:

Half the day hazy with the previous night.
The non-drinker drinking, non-smoker smoking.
Two or three men, two or three girls.
The red coated waiters of Harbour Bar.
The redlight district dancer at the Apollo Room.
The foreigners and the foreign-returned.
The expensive menu and the shadow of Marx.
The Biryani Hyderabadi and the sighs for Bangla Desh.
The see-through dress and the show nothing sari.
The fog in the head and the sense of success.
The music Indian and the language English.
The Sindhi Sales Manager and the Parsi Fashion Model. (*CP* 232)

In the same poem, Ezekiel describes Indian mentality in a satirical tone with the contradictory statements:

No Indian whisky Sir all imported this is Taj.
Yes Sir soda is Indian Sir.
Midnight.
Taxi strike. George Fernandes.

Long walk to Churchgate between pavement sleepers.
Last train to Borivli, stopping at all stations.
Two blind beggars, husband and wife, in the first class compartment.
Half the day hazy with the previous night. (*CP* 232)

In his *Latter-Day Psalms*, creating a very Indian flavor, Ezekiel's devotion to Indian writing in English is unique. His poems "The Patriot" and "The Professor" from *Very Indian Poems in Indian English* try to reflect Indian ethos and culture by describing the characteristic Indian attitude in so-called *Swadeshi Angrezi*. These poems depict the syntactical oddities of English used by Indian speakers. "These poems imitate the idiolect features of English used by Gujarati speakers. Some of these features are also present in other Indian language: the use of the present progressive tense for the simple present tense, un-English collocation of lexical items, and literal translation of phrases and idioms" (Parthasarathy 8).

Ezekiel exposes the common Indian mistake of using present progressive tense instead of the simple present tense. In his poem "The Patriot", he uses faulty English:

I am standing for peace and non-violence.
Why world is fighting fighting
Why all people of world
Are not following Mahatma Gandhi,
I am simply not understanding.
Ancient Indian Wisdom is 100% correct.
I should say even 200% correct. (*CP* 237)

Ezekiel has created humour by using faulty English to depict characteristic Indian attitude. Indeed, Ezekiel's poetic genius has unique potential to create a complete Indian atmosphere by capturing the very Indian ethos and culture. Here he describes the glory of Ancient India and deplores the fact that new generation does not believe in the teachings of Mahatma Gandhi. Further, he points out the mistakes of Indians while speaking as "100%" correct, even "200%" correct. Besides his use of *Babu Angrezi*, his faulty use of indefinite articles, his use of "no" to enforce a point and the repetition of a word to stress the point create the atmosphere of Indianness.

The poem also shows the spell of the poet's use of irony. The reproduction of tone, idiom and voice, colloquialism like *goonda* fellow throwing stones at Indirabehn create humour and expresses the Indian ethos and culture. To respect elders and masters is one of the excellent ethos and culture of Indians, which is evident in the line: "Friends, Romans, countrymen, I am saying (to myself) / Lend me the ears" (*CP* 237). The poet very skillfully refers the famous line from William Shakespeare's *Julius Caesar*. By quoting Shakespeare, Ezekiel pays tribute to the greatest dramatist of the World. In this poem, the poet also throws light on fashion and foreign things, which are blindly followed by new generation. He says:

> You want one glass lassi?
> Very good for digestion.
> With little salt lovely drink,
> Better than wine; (*CP* 238)

Usually it is a common Indian attitude towards drinking. He talks of Indian drink *lassi*, which is better for health than the foreign wine.

As an Indian, the poet is also interested to draw the ethos and culture of Indians towards neighbouring countries. In the same poem, he says, "Pakistan behaving like this / China behaving like that / It is making me very sad, I am telling you" (*CP* 238). Ezekiel very artistically reflects the cultural ethos of Indians toward the national integration. He has revealed not only what many Indians think, but also the way they think in English in the lines from the same poem:

> All men are brothers, no?
> In India also
> Gujaraties, Maharashtrians, Hindiwallahas

All brothers
Though some are having funny habits.
Still, you tolerate me,
I tolerate you,
One day, Ram Rajya is surely coming. (*CP* 238)

Ezekiel's idea of *Ram Rajya* shows his closeness to Indianness. He speaks of brotherhood, which is rooted in ancient Indian glory. Despite domestic walls of caste, colour and religion, he tries to build universal brotherhood. Undoubtedly, this is the most striking feature of Indian ethos and culture.

Moreover, Ezekiel attempts to create Indian flavour by using common Hindi words in his poetry. *Indirabehn, goonda fellow, lassi, Ram Rajya, Hindiwallahas, Guru, Ashram, Burka, Chapati, pan, mantra* are some of the vernacular words the poet has used to make Indian life more real. Thus, in his attempt to reflect cultural ethos through the use of vernacular words and imagery drawn from the common situations in India is successful.

In "The Professor," Ezekiel has crossed the limit of using *Babu Angrezi* as commonly used by some Indians. He has broken the rules of idiom and grammar in the lines from "The Professor," "If you are coming again this side by chance / Visit please my humble residence also / I am living just on opposite house's backside" (*CP* 239).

Ezekiel speaks of an old age in the same poem. He looks at old age seriously from intellectual point of view. He thinks of sons and his family after retirement. A retired man can understand his limitations in the era of changing values and lifestyle. The poet presents the pain of old age and life:

...health is O.K. Usual aches and pains.
No diabetes, no blood pressure, no heart attack.
This is because of sound habits in youth.
.....
This year I am sixty-nine

and hope to score century.
You were so thin, like stick,
Now you are man of weight and consequence.
That is good joke. (*CP* 239)

The poet seems to seek meaning and purpose in human life. It comes to man after too much experience of life. Indians believe in prayer and worship especially in their old age when they understand life from very close:

> It appears that Nissim Ezekiel looks at an old age life of an Indian rather amusingly. He probably infers that Indians after retiring from active life do not wield a philosophic view of life. It is an enormous perception. If a retired man looks after the social obligations that too amount to prayers and worship. It also adds meaning and purpose. In joint families, it was required as this was also considered a cultural heritage of India which taught to worship and love man. This kind of life does add purpose and meaning. Only that it requires an eye to observe delicate nice good things of life in relations otherwise important for life. (Prem 123)

Ezekiel has also depicted a common Indian situation in "Dead end Story" of the rift between the mother-in-law and daughter-in-law wherein one can study the cultural ethos of the two women regarding their domestic relationship:

Typical Indian mother-in-law
to the bride
returning from her honeymoon,
"Don't worry, dear,
I need no help in the kitchen
Leave it to me, please."
Then she complained
to her husband and son,
"That girl is no help to me
in the kitchen, is she?"

Said the modern, 'advanced' bride,
"I won't take it.
Either she lets me help her
in the kitchen or she must's complain
that I don't help her in the kitchen". (*CP* 292)

The Indian family life, full of quarrels of in-laws, is commonly described by the poet:

Said the son
To his angry bride,
'if you quarrel with my Mother,
You quarrel with me.' (*CP* 292)

In fact, everyone is responsible for this degradation, which leads him or her in a strange dilemma. They are wondering between two extremes—one is loss of peace and other is cheerfulness of materialistic achievements. The poet voices the situation in his poem "From Edinburgh Interlude":

From the life of cheerful degradation
normal in my neighborhood,
I thought I had escaped...
I have become
Part of the scene
Which I can neither Love nor hate. (*CP* 289)

This can be a best example of degradation of man from human to dragon which is emphatically presented in "An Atheist Speaks": "If you look into a mirror / it's the devil reflected / and god remote" (*CP* 288). In short, Ezekiel's point of view is clear to maintain a balance in life. He tries to achieve redemption of man:

> His portrayal of the times and climes, of life, and strife, at low-mimetic level is captivating and contemplative. He has brought out the crisis in all its nakedness for the treatment of earthly life, and for therapeutic purpose, through catharsis because he is concerned with the

> meaning and significance of the life, and the creation. He has presented the life, attitudes and the whole environment in such a way that the experience becomes at once local as well as universal. (Verma 171)

Most of Indians are credulous and superstitious by nature. They are after faith-cure. In "Healers," Ezekiel provides a kind of remedial approach and tries to suggest a meditative attitude to recover from the situation:

> God's love remains your heritage.
> You need not change
> your way of life.
> Know your mantra, meditate,
> release your Kundalini,
> get your Shakti Awakening
> and float with the spirit
> to your destination. (*CP* 232)

Here, the poet deliberately employs Indian words *mantra, kundalini, shakti* in order to grace authenticity to the content. The 'healers' provide the secret of all 'cures'. They prescribe the same kind of cure for all. In this poem, the poet seems to be a wide reader of religious philosophy. In this respect G. Nageswar Rao remarks:

> In a general sense one may describe his work as that of a religious philosophical poet. He is widely read and except for Islam, one finds a pervading spirit of such different religion as Buddhism, Zen, Hinduism and Christianity in his poetry and the basic simplicities of living throughout the poetry of Ezekiel appear to be his deep moral need. A desire to live life on nature's terms is almost out of the reach of only modern man, particularly the urban sophisticated man. The only possibility is to live a sane life in accordance with the basic simplicities of human nature: frankness, honesty, simplicity, truth, friendship tenderness and love and patiently to build a life with these. (162)

Perhaps Ezekiel is the first Indian poet who does not forget to reflect corrupt, hypocritical, apathetic and indifferent attitude of common person through the treatment of the issues like the poverty, the squalor, the anguish and the irony of Indian existence in his poetry. His readers have a moral and intellectual impact of Ezekiel's description of vivid and ironical vignettes. However, his poetry is characterized by the exact and concrete picture of irony, compassion, human concern and urge for better and happier life. "Ezekiel is a psychologist of sort. He is rather fond of analyzing the devious ways in which the human mind works. Hence, he has unusual interest in depicting the portraits of individual human beings" (Karnani 169).

In this phase, *Hymns in Darkness* shows spiritual and metaphysical concerns which he has derived from basic Hindu scriptures in the poems like "The Egoist's Prayer" and the Hymns. This is a collective result of his rootedness in the land. It seems that Ezekiel's intellectual ability even in his growing age is astonishing in its richness in order to compose such masterpieces on religious sensibility and spirituality. Fortunately, it is in this age that Ezekiel can accept failures and frustration of his surrounding humanity with a big heart. His mood in this collection is one of reverence and submission. This mood of complete surrender to realities of life serves as a tribute to Indian spirituality by the poet which may not be useless for the coming generation.

Latter-Day Psalms shows the imperialistic influence of nationalism in the form of nativism. This impact of imperialism got suppressed by the growing culture of Marathas especially in Maharashtra. The Psalms are basically folklores from Bible contributed their charms to generations. On the other hand, these psalms are written when there was nothing to read and write. In that hour, Ezekiel read *Gideon Bible*. In fact, the composition shows the impact of Bible having no relevance to contemporary consciousness in India. Therefore, these psalms need to be appropriated so that a compromising result could be explored to seek God. Though the Psalms differs from the cultural standpoint of India, they reflect Ezekiel is a humanist having touch for man's weaknesses. "Despite questioning the sincerity of the Psalmist's feelings, he admires them because they are human creations, destined to be flowed and incomplete" (Sharma 147).

However, the poems like "The Patriot," and "The Professor" treated as a satire on lapses in Indian societal practices. In "The Patriot," the poet brings the human weaknesses by exposing the follies of half imperialistic fever infected Indians. While in "The Professor," Ezekiel focuses the unhappiness of the teaching community. In this regard Bijay Kumar Das finds out:

> Ezekiel not only recreates Indian characters in their situation but he recreates the language as well. The tone may appear to be mocking as the poet becomes an ironist or even a parodist but he faithfully recreates these characters as they appear in their real life. Ezekiel's friendliness and sympathy with the poor and common people redeem his poetry from being caricatures of people. (82)

Ezekiel's most significant contribution seems his treatment of friendliness and sympathy with the poor and common man in his poetry as discussed in this chapter. He tries to expose Indian attitude of a common man from the experiences of real life through various themes. He focuses their typical, superstitious, traditional, patriotic, organizational, religious, social, political, psychological attitudes which help to express Indian ethos and culture in his poetry. Moreover, his recurring themes of love and sex, man-woman relationship, religious-philosophical strain, human failure and so on bring forth cultural ethos of Indians. All these factors render him a position of a critic of Indian society. In fact, the overall discussion in this chapter confirms its aptness in terms of reflection of Indian ethos and culture in Ezekiel's recent phase of poetry.

Works Cited

Abidi, S.Z.H. *Studies in Indo Anglian Poetry.* Bareilly: Prakash Book Depot, 1978, 291. Print.

Chindhade, Shirish. *Five Indian English Poets.* New Delhi: Atlantic Publishers and Distributors, 2009, 41-47. Print.

Daruwalla, Keki N. *Collected Poems 1970-2005.* New Delhi: Penguin Books, 2006, 74-102. Print.

Das, Bijay Kumar. *The Horizon of Nissim Ezekiel's Poetry.* New Delhi: B.K. Publishing Corporation, 1995. 82, Print.

Ezekiel, Nissim. *Collected Poems.* New Delhi: O.U.P., 2005. Text. All subsequent references to Ezekiel's poems shall be from this edition.

Jussawalla, Adil. *New Poetry, Reading in Commonwealth Literature,* ed. William Walsh., 1973. 77. Print.

Karnani, Chetan. *Nissim Ezekiel.* New Delhi, Arnold Hemingway 1974, 142-69. Print.

King, Bruce. *Three Indian Poets.* Madras: Oxford, 1991, 48. Print.

Kumar, Satish. *A Survey of Indian English Poetry.* Bareilly: Prakash Book Depot, 2001, 218. Print.

Kurup, P.K.J. *Contemporary Indian Poetry in English.* New Delhi: Atlantic Publishers and Distributors, 1991, 88-101. Print.

Mahan, Shaila. *The Poetry of Nissim Ezekiel.* Jaipur: Classic, 2001, 47. Print.

Mahapatra, Jayant. *The Lie of Dawns Poems 1974-2008.* New Delhi: Authors Press, 2009, 46. Print.

Mishra, Rajendra Nath. "Post-Independence Anguish in Nissim Ezekiel's Poetry." *Contemporary Indian Literature in English, A Humanistic Perspective.* Ed. Mithilesh K. Pandey. New Delhi: Kalyani P., 1999, 11-12. Print.

Mishra, Sanjit. *The Poetic Art of Nissim Ezekiel.* New Delhi: Atlantic Publishers and Distributors, 2001, 99-129. Print.

Mokashi-Punekar, Shankar. *Theoretical and Practical Studies in Indo-English Literature.* Dharwad: Karnatak U., 1978, 18. Print.

Nandy, Pritish. Ed. *Indian Poetry in English Today.* New Delhi: Sterling Paperbacks, 1973, 9. Print.

Parthasarathy, R. ed. *Ten Twentieth-Century Indian Poets.* New Delhi: O.U.P., 1976, 8. Print.

Patil, Suresh Pandurang. "Nissim Ezekiel: A Poet of Social Conscience." *Galaxy: International Multidisciplinary Research Journal* 2.1 (April 2012): 1-4. Print.

Prem, P.C.K. *English Poetry in India: A Comprehensive Survey of Trends and Thought Patterns.* New Delhi: Authors Press, 2011, 117-23. Print.

Ramanujan, A.K. *Collected Poems.* Delhi: OUP, 1997, 34-251. Text.

Rao, G. Nageswar. *Essays on Nissim Ezekiel.* Ed. T.R. Sharma, Meerut: Shalabh, 1994, 162. Print.

Shahane, V.A. "The Religious Philosophical Strain in Nissim Ezekiel's Poetry." *Perspective on Nissim Ezekiel.* Ed. S.C. Dwivedi. Allahabad: K.M. Agencies 1989, 22. Print.

_______. "The Religious-Philosophical Strain in Nissim Ezekiel". *Journal of South Asian Literature* (Spring-Summer 1976): 254. Print.

Sharma, Sushil Kumar. "Fourteen Questions to Nissim Ezekiel." Ed. T.R. Sharma. *Essays on Nissim Ezekiel.* Meerut: Shalabh Prakashan, 1994, 147. Print.

Tilak, Raghukul. *New Indian English Poets and Poetry.* New Delhi: Rama Brothers, 1995, 34-5. Print.

Verma, Priti. "Crisis and Redemption: Therapeutic Canvas of Nissim Ezekiel's Poetry". *The Indian Journal of English Studies* xliv (2007): 171. Print.

6 Conclusion

This final chapter is concerned with bringing together the salient points that have emerged in the present book. After analyzing extensively, it has been observed that Nissim Ezekiel is an Indian poet. In his wide range of poetry, Indian ethos and culture is reflected throughout. It is proved that he is a typical Indian poet by blood and soul. In order to prove Ezekiel's Indianness and study reflection of Indian ethos and culture in his poetry, primary and secondary sources have been referred to.

In his early phase of poetic career, Ezekiel's poetry reveals his juvenile approach to life and state of immaturity towards perfection. An image of a pagan woman and man-woman relationship towards sex and love are his favorite themes. This impact is clearly seen in his verse collection like *Early Poems* (1945), *A Time to Change* (1952), *Sixty Poems* (1953), and *The Third* (1959). In these collections, the poet tries to reveal cultural ethos of Indians through the treatment of physical dimensions of the relationship between man and woman.

On the other hand, *The Unfinished Man* (1960) and *The Exact Name* (1965) bring his humanistic approach to real Indian situations. He pictures the shades of urban ethos, culture, tradition, blind beliefs, superstitions, and societal aspects. It seems that he wants to bring about a cultural reform in Indian society. Ezekiel paints this picture of Indian society through various images, irony, humour and satire. Therefore, it is possible to call him a critic of Indian society.

In *A Time to Change*, his poem "To A Certain Lady" gives an account of domestic life of the philosophical realization between husband and wife. The poem explains that shouting is a way of expressing love. On the other hand, the poet gives character sketch of Indian wives and their ways of nagging. The lady nags the husband when he is nothing willing to agree to her buying an expensive lipstick. Thus, in Ezekiel's poetry the Indian wives are generally very demanding and the husbands find it difficult to satisfy.

Ezekiel's early poetry is predominated with the theme of love and sex. This might be because of his full bloom of youth. Naturally, his heart was full of love and sex. In his poem "And God Revealed" the poet dwells on the peculiarity of earthly love with its total absorption in the chosen physical organs. The pagan woman stands for existence of sex and emotion in the heart and the soul of the poet. The poem expresses that our redemption is possible only if guilt is confessed. There is a strong feeling that consolation dwells in love and poetry. Such a broad view of love can maintain the relationship between man and woman. Therefore, the poem asserts that human relationship and marital happiness bring fulfillment in life.

A Time to Change voices the romantic misery of the tortured self of Ezekiel which makes him to realize his concern for morality and meaning of life. Here, Ezekiel tries to synthesize the secular and the religious through releasing modern man from the ethical anxieties. In fact, the title itself suggests the idea that the time has come to bring about a change in present human life which appears far away from rooted Indian ethos and culture:

> "A Time to Change" is the point at which the moral self gathers the awareness that if the paradoxes posed by the putrid city, the pagan-woman and the religious-philosophical quest of the self have to maintain a certain rhythm with one another a change in the perception has to be effected. It needs the poetic self to caution the voyager's moral self that it is "A Time to Change". (Kurup 35)

Sixty Poems and *The Third* deal with the issues of the ethical anxiety and the sins committed by man. Here, the poet is aware of his sins and accepts the truth that "Man is measure of mankind". In "Prayer I," the poet is captured between the morality and the force of temptation. Poems like "Situation," "Marriage Poems," "Two Nights of Love" and "The Old Abyss" are under the category of poems of body which reveal that the company of woman is helpful to make marital life easy. While in poems like "Encounter," "At the Party" and "At the Hotel," the woman is portrayed as a seductress. Thus, the poet reflects the ethos and culture of Indians who are captured between the morality and the sense of temptation.

The Unfinished Man presents a realistic approach to a peculiar ethos, neither confronted nor envisaged so far. "Urban" is a remarkable poem for it tells about the city man who is caught up in the phantasmagoria of sex and power from where there is no redemption:

> The person in this poem is passionately attached to the city and its worn-out tracks of custom and habit. He is always at a great distance from the "hills" which symbolize the loftiness of spirit. His river of life is dry, and the winds lie dead in his path meaning that he is devoid of the creative breath which has the power of regeneration. He does not perceive the rebirth of the skies such morning nor does he feel the reclining fingers of the shadows of the night on his eyes. In other words, he does not experience the life-death continuum within himself. There is no place for the sun and the rain in his closed system indicating that he lacks light or warmth, as well as the fertilizing power of creativity. (Kher 3-7)

Thus, another poem "Morning Walk" gives details about the city of Bombay. The poem makes aware of spiritual decay due to unwanted growth of slums. Ezekiel is a modern poet by virtue of the time. He writes about the 'every man'. But his main concern being a modern poet is his representation of certain urban ethos, the environment, thought, sentiments of the essential man behind the modern urban man. It denotes that modern man makes efforts to search something new by breaking from traditional values. But, instead of searching new, he gets captured with spiritual decay. "Nissim Ezekiel's poems are the records of the moral aches and pains of a modern Indian in one of his own cities" (Jussawalla 79).

In his poem "Enterprise," a unique effort to build 'unity in diversity' is made, but unfortunately, tradition-bound attitude of the society does not allow it. A group of people set a supreme goal, but because of their usual attitude to quarrel over trifle thing led them to a dead end. Though the situation in this poem marks the break up from Indian ethos and culture, the human soul tries to escape from this spiritual degradation:

> A recurring note in his poetry is the wound urban civilization inflicts on unattached man. His poetry gives the impression of an oversensitive soul caught in the tentacles of a cruel city civilization, unable to escape from its vagaries and consequently developing a love-hate relationship with its torment. (Khanna 594)

The reflection of urban ethos is unique in Ezekiel's poetry. It is accepted that no contemporary poet has captured a more comprehensive picture of the metropolitan life than Ezekiel has done. "Ezekiel has identified himself completely with Indian, and more particularly with the city of Bombay, and this identification sustains him as a writer and as a human being" (Varma 170).

The fourth volume *Exact Name* offers an aesthetic solution to all the unresolved, moral, psychological and theological paradoxes of life. It is in this volume that Ezekiel seems more mature through experiences in real life. As a result of it, he does not spare to describe superstitious attitude of Indians. In "Night of the Scorpion," he tries to focus the superstitions followed by the Indians. He involves all the community in case of scorpion biting. All the operations are served to minimize the agony. However, his main concern is to highlight the superstitious mind of the villagers. On the other hand, he emphasizes the voice of a sceptic and rationalist father who is compelled to practice superstitions. Thus, he reflects the overwhelming mass ethos and culture of villagers. Besides, sketching the ethos of Indian mother, Ezekiel peeps into the heart of mother in the poem. He glorifies maternal love and affection for children. This definitely reminds of the typical mother of Indian folklore.

Nissim tries to bring the ethos and culture of the villagers in "Night of the Scorpion". The villagers are God fearing folk. They surrender themselves to the will of God and consider that everything is decided and executed by Him. They prepare themselves that the priest is most nearer to God. In the poem, they call the priest in order to minimize the pain of the mother through rituals. Bringing out the ethos and culture of the Indians, Omana Antony puts:

> Indian tradition is rich in spiritual myths and ideologies. The belief in the previous birth and the next birth, and the relevance of the 'karma' and the consequent sufferings in the present life forms the basic concept of Hindu mythology in Indian background. It is this belief that warns humans to abstain from evil. And this belief in its full strength is practiced among the villagers. (52)

However, Ezekiel seems to be settled down in India and its environment as it clearly reflected in his volume *The Exact Name*. This makes him more confident to reflect Indian ethos and culture in his recent phase of poetry.

In his recent phase of verse—*Poster Poems* (1969), *Hymns in Darkness* (1976), *Latter-Day Psalms* (1982), and the Latest Poems in *Collected Poems* (1989)—Ezekiel seems more mature and spiritual. His recent verse is marked with the themes like Religio-philosophic strain, characteristics Indian attitude, man-woman relationship, love and sex. His earlier phase reveals these shades to some extent. But, Ezekiel here tries to bring it with a humanistic perspective of reality.

He defends his right to be considered Indian as explained in his poem "Background, Casually". He expresses the humiliation and victimization from those belonging to other culture. Finally, the poet declares that India is the place where he belongs. This note gives his identity as an Indian. The perspectives presented in these poems seem comforting in a way, and offering political support. Being Indian, the poet can present authentic picture of Indian society.

In *Hymns in Darkness*, the poet tries to bring out the weaknesses of humankind through the portraits of various characters from Indian society. Ezekiel points out the changing ethos and culture of lover and beloved in India. He exposes the seductive attitude of woman. Once upon a time, woman was worshipped as Goddess. She was the epitome of shyness then. But she has changed her culture and became seductive as presented in his poems like "Three Women" and "Motives". The poet expresses the changed tendency of woman to force the man for sexual union. At the same time, the poet also depicts the changed attitude of Indian man to treat woman as a sex object.

Ezekiel in his poem "Guru," describes the Indian saints of modern times to expose their separation from traditional values. Indians have been worshipping their saints since ancient times. Indians have lot of faith and respect for their saints. However, dealing with modern saints, Ezekiel tries to bring forth their hypocritical attitude. In this respect, he not only comments on the attitude of modern saints, but also criticizes the slavish Indian attitude of the people who worship them blindly. In short, the poet shows that the modern civilization is under clutches of devaluation and degradation. "The recurring note in Ezekiel's recent poems is the hurt that urban civilization inflicts on modern man, dehumanizing him, and subjecting his verities to pollution and devaluation" (Iyengar 660). While revealing the deceiving attitude of the so-called *sadhus*, Ezekiel seems an authentic Indian poet for a real Indian can only reach the soul of its people.

Ezekiel, with his keen, sharp and penetrating eyes, observes husband–wife relationship. In "Servant," the poet concentrates on typically suppressed Indian wife. The wife is innocent, as she does not protest when her husband beats her. She is unaware of her rights. She bears all types of sufferings with open eyes. Ezekiel also travels through the Indian homes and finds out Indian life is full of crisis. In "Dead End Story," Ezekiel captures the rift between the mother-in-law and daughter-in-law that occurs in every Indian family. It reveals the domestic Indian ethos and culture of the both women. Ezekiel's intention behind reflecting the cultural ethos of characters from Indian families serves as remedy. "Ezekiel's deliberate dig at the urbanized modern sophisticated families proves to be therapeutic in effect" (Mohanty 91).

Ezekiel's poetry acquires an unmistakable Indian ethos and culture. His use of so-called *Swadeshi Angrezi* in his poetry depicts the characteristic Indian attitude. He exposes the Indians in their use of the syntactical oddities of English. This is obvious in his poems *Very Indian Poems in Indian English* where he uses present progressive tense instead of simple present tense in order to bring forth the characteristic Indian attitude. Here Ezekiel not only uses the faulty English, but also expresses the way the people think in English. This shows his minute observation of Indians and their cultural ethos:

> He represents the truly Indian with his deep involvement in spiritual and intellectual satisfaction by rooting himself in the physical and the social atmosphere. In his social growth, he could hardly keep himself aloof from the social problems. His commitment to India and his attachment with the environment seem to be the main source of his inspiration for writing poetry. Though Ezekiel was accused of being 'a poet of a local habitation and a name', of only being restricted to the city of Bombay, yet he seems to have broad and deep sympathy for the human race as a whole. (Patil 1)

Ezekiel has exposed the Indian life with all its manifold aspects. "In poems after poems, he expresses his concern for humanity and tries to find out what ails mankind and to get out of it" (Das, "Nissim Ezekiel's Humanistic Poetry: An Overview" 3). He explained in one of his interviews, "Politics, social life, civic problems, education, economic difficulties, cultural, dilemmas are all part of my daily life; I would like that identification to be fully expressed in my poetry" (Chindhade 57). It is through these aspects, he has made efforts to explore the Indian ethos and culture. Ezekiel, in his recent verse *Hymns in Darkness*, discusses the societal and cultural aspects of India with contemporary situation and case studies. In this manner:

> He desires to achieve complete identity with self. Family and society and god, several of his poems, reveal his increased awareness of Indian social milieu and Ezekiel is seen to be a very Indian poet in English. Fake healers Sadhu, saints all are intrinsic part of Indian social life and these are treated ironically and satirically in number of poems in Hymns in Darkness. (Pastapure 1).

Nissim seems to be first Indian poet to trace various Indian milieus in his poetry. As a modern poet of India, he has voiced experiences of the common man through his own thoughts and experiences. He suggests other Indian poets that there should be synthesis between the ancient and modern culture. He shares it in an interview with Anees Jung that "The problems of Indian writers are strange. They have to make a synthesis between the ancient and modern culture" (Jung 12). Ezekiel makes a beautiful fusion of Jewish and Indian, western and Indian and also of ancient and modern in his poetry. His poetry reveals ordinariness of things and events and keeps a pace with the changing scene of the international trends. He thinks that poetry must reflect the time it is written "in relation of the writer to his age". In fact, Indian English poetry began during British rule in India; consequently it reflects great connection with international happenings.

Ezekiel's most significant contribution to his poetry is his treatment of versification, imagery, symbolism and use of irony, satire, humour etc. It is with the help of such devices, he brings forth Indian ethos and culture in his poetry. In this sense, Ezekiel proves that he is a perfect crafts man of his poetry. Most of his contemporary Indian English poets adhere to no specific form or genre of poetry. There are variations in visual shapes, size, and sentence structure in their poetry. The better part of Ezekiel's poetic genius is verse libre. This new form defies the classical verse forms. It encourages natural speech and liberates the rigid pattern of stanza. Ezekiel's poetry is marked with simplicity in language and diction. The use of irony is one of the most outstanding features of Ezekiel's poetry. In his poem "Background, Casually," the poet uses irony to achieve comic effects and hits target of criticism. Actually, irony, wit, humour, mockery and satire are inseparable from each other. He uses these devices in his *Very Indian Poems in Indian English* to bring the real picture of human beings from Indian society.

Ezekiel weaves vivid and picturesque images from different sources. The images of coldness, rottenness, dimness, sickness, clamour and burning passions are used to reveal Indian ethos and culture in his poetry. In the words of Bijay Kumar Das:

> Ezekiel incorporates the heat and dust, the sun and the floods, the sense of poverty and deprivation into the texture of his moods. The images of 'India' pervade although his poetry. The changing reality of love and the human relationship on the one hand and the unchanging contours of Indian landscape on the other are as it were the *spiritus mundi* from where he draws all his images. (Das, "Imagery in the Poetry of Nissim Ezekiel" 20)

Ezekiel's poetry is marked with 'intellectualism'—another aspect of modern poetry. Life is seen from the point of view of wholeness, intellectual and spiritual maturity in Ezekiel's poetry. In a way, he suggests how to live happily, calmly, and ethically as an integrated human being. In his recent volume

Latter-Day Psalms, like other modern poets, Ezekiel often refers the word 'God' without being very religious himself. It becomes the issue of study if the 'God' mentioned in his poem is Jew, or Hindu or Christian. After analyzing, it comes to know that his 'God' is familiar like a friend. His God is common to all. He sometimes praises God and sometimes accuses Him. He communicates his feelings of anger, praise and frustration. How can I breathe freely if thou breakest the teeth of the ungodly? (*CP* 253).

However, Nissim Ezekiel paints the characters and their ethos and culture from the situations in real Indian life. In this respect K.R.S. Iyengar points out that his poetry is "splendidly evocative and satisfyingly sensuous" (Iyengar 657). Thus he is proved to be a genuine Indian poet writing in English. In this way, the scent of Indian ethos and culture lingers through every character and situation in his poetry. The various facets of Indian environment reflected in his poetry do not leave any way to call him alienated or rootless. In fact, his willingness establishes relationship with the human situation around him and appreciates him as an Indian poet.

Indeed, Ezekiel's poetry reveals that he is alienated from the core of Indian ethos, but he tries to remain attached to India and its society till the last moment of his life. On the other hand, he spent most of his life in the city of Bombay. The city seems to be influenced by western culture to some extent. The atmosphere of the city suited to his lifestyle. In fact, his association and disassociation from India, makes him a critic of Indian society. He observes every aspect of Indian society from the close as expressed in almost all his poetry. His poetry reveals that his poetic career is covered with Indian ethos and culture. He is influenced by other major poets, but he himself made efforts to solve his problems and to provide impartial answer to the questions of his readers.

Ezekiel's attempt to observe minutely the Indian ethos and culture through various societal aspects is outstanding:

> To sum up Ezekiel, in his own way, tried to express the Indian ethos and culture through making other people know that he is capable of adapting different elements in his poetry. His aspiration has been to give expression to the genius of the soul of India, to support this he never showed any interest to go and settle abroad. He has been the poet of the city and Bombay made himself known as a minority and remained rooted in that metropolitan soil. Except for a short period of few spells, he always remained in India and said that his backward place is where he is. (Wesly and Chandra 13)

Ezekiel really seems to be true representative of Indian society as his themes are chosen from almost all walks of life. The aim behind selecting the poet for the present study is to discuss the reflection of continuous quest for self and Indian cultural ethos in his poetry. He deals with his own experiences through themes like superstitions, blind beliefs, urban India, man-woman relationship, love and sex, illusion with religion and spirituality and the disillusionment. Making life happy without breaking old morals and values is a striking feature of Ezekiel's poetry. Being modern, the poet feels dissatisfied with the existing morals, social and religious values. Though he wrote poetry satirically on domestic quarrels, the poet was dissatisfied with the depicted codes and conducts of married life.

On the contrary, some critics are not happy with the manner Ezekiel has explained the Hindu lads and their parents in his poem "Background, Casually". V.M. Madge is listed first among such critics. In his article "Pride and Prejudice in Ezekiel's Poetry," Madge says, "First, it is not quite clear why the bullying is being communalized. It is quite significant and revealing that the school boy identifies his tormentors not by their names, as any school boy would normally do, but by their communities" (Madge 188). Secondly, "Especially 'strong and undernourished' goes much beyond its brief and comments on Hindu parents" (Madge 189).

Madge adds, "In Healers', once again, the stress is on Hindu quacks, as if hypocritical shepherds do not exist in India luring the lamb into the arms of the loving saviour" (Madge 190). Madge also makes an interesting comment:

> If in the 19th century, India was a land of snakes, tigers and maharajahs to the foreigners, to the non resident aliens like Naipaul and to the resident ones like Ezekiel, in the 20th century, India has acquired a new stereotype of being the land of "beggars, hawkers, pavement sleepers, hutment dwellers and slums," as if there are no Shantiniketans, Dhvanyalokas, IITs and IISCs. (192)

The following comment of Suresh Patil may help to answer the objections raised by Madge. Patil says:

> His theory of poetry is "that every poet knows what it is to be delighted with the poem he has written, while at the same time to feel the misery at the thought that a better poem was sacrificed to it". His new modern poetry is steeped with irony, skeptical attitude, restrained emotions, and critical self-consciousness and with an intellectual purpose. His primary concern is not oriental India which abounds with the Maharajas, snake-charmers, sadhus and magicians with supernatural powers but truly India. Though Jewish by birth, he never disclaims his linkage with India. (1)

G.J.V. Prasad also passes an interesting and objecting comment on Ezekiel's most famous line, "My backward place is where I am". He says:

> Being neither an NRI nor foreign educated; the lines irritated me as a young man but not anymore. I did then, object to the description of India as a backward place. And for god's sake he lives in Bombay, the commercial capital of the country! Older, but perhaps not wiser, I realize the value and weight of those simple lines—it is not that India is backward—that is a truism, but that one can serve best where one has a sense of belonging, a place one call home, backward though it may be. (Prasad 499)

Ezekiel's continuous quest for an Indian identity throughout his poetry is itself a reply to the objections raised against him. Ezekiel considers India his home and therefore a whole family. He may play a significant role of a family member having the rights to points out the follies and lacunas in Indian scenes in order to rectify and reform it. In this manner, Ezekiel plays an important part of a social reformer to correct the social ills coming across the way of inculcating and maintaining the significance of the Indian ethos and culture.

However, the certain objections raised by the above critics may find their answers in the following observations put by Ezekiel himself. Ezekiel asserts:

> I am not supporting the touchiness and nationalistic chauvinism which is evoked when a culture is criticized in a literary work. Even a stereotype has its real roots, in a country and a culture, a class and a religion, a profession and a way of life. Even a prejudice in literature is valuable when its causes are probed and the frequency of its occurrence examined. No literature worth the name is wholly impartial and objective, whether or not it deals with cross-cultural situations. Some distinctions are clearly necessary in assessing the national, cultural, class, religious and other major or incidental meaning of a literary work as drawn out and defined conceptually. (qtd. in Anklesaria 184)

Although, Ezekiel appears to be satiric and making fun of certain Indian attitudes and belief system, he is never without sympathy for Indians. He extensively concerned about the quagmire of poverty, spiritual decay, seductive attitude of woman and corruption etc. It appears that Ezekiel loves India and its people as he continuously pleads for his Indian identity. He accepts Indians with all their weaknesses and lacunas. Sometimes, he laughs at Indians and their ways of living in order to bring about a change in their attitude, ethos and culture by insulting them. It seems different technique of Ezekiel to bring changes in Indians. He observes their proud attitude and ways of reacting to an insult. Thus, Ezekiel proves his concern of a social reformer coming in terms of Indian ethos and culture.

Indeed, Ezekiel seems to be more careful about the common man in his poetry than his contemporaries. In this regard, Bijay Kumar Das puts:

> Ezekiel is a great humanist poet. It is in this aspect that Ezekiel excels most of his contemporaries. The concern for the common man wherever he may be, gives Ezekiel's poetry a kind of authenticity and liveliness which at once distinguishes him from others. He is aware of the need of a common man. (*The Horizon of Nissim Ezekiel's Poetry* 19)

To be fair to Ezekiel, apart from the charges against him, a concrete evaluation of his poetic contribution should be taken in consideration from the point of view of percolation of Indian ethos and culture in his poetry. In his writings, poems, interviews and Radio talk he is seen attached to modern India. His modern view of India has been continuously seen in struggling with the historical and cultural past. In this sense, he appears to be a critic of Indian society. Perhaps very few poets of his times are successful in presenting India with such an extraordinary and rich cultural reality of humanity as Ezekiel has been. It never occurs that Ezekiel's presentation of India is merely for the sake of writing poetry.

The present investigation of Ezekiel's poetry is undertaken into two phases—the early and the recent. In his earlier phase of poetry, Ezekiel reveals fascination for romantic mood and the reality of the environment while exposing Indian cultural ethos. While in his recent phase, Ezekiel's humanistic and spiritual approach to reform Indian society is surmounting in his poetry. Ultimately, in the present research, it is found that Ezekiel is deeply rooted in India and its ethos and culture. He could possess a unique position of a legend and a mentor to growing writers in his lifetime. In short, Ezekiel secures a prominent place among his contemporaries in percolating Indian ethos and culture in his poetry.

Works Cited

Anklesaria, Havovi. Ed. "Cross-Cultural Encounter in Literature". *Nissim Ezekiel Remembered.* New Delhi: Sahitya Akademi, 2008, 184. Print.

Antony, Omana. "Indianism in Nissim Ezekiel: A Study of Night of the Scorpion, The Professor and The Patriot." *Litsearch.* 2.2 (June 2012): 52. Print.

Chindhade, Shirish. *Five English Poets.* New Delhi: Atlantic Publishers, 2001, 57. Print.

Das, Bijay Kumar. *The Horizon of Nissim Ezekiel's Poetry.* New Delhi: B.K. Publishing Corporation, 1995, 19. Print.

______. "Imagery in the Poetry of Nissim Ezekiel." *Perspectives on Nissim Ezekiel.* Ed. S.C. Dwivedi. New Delhi: Kitab Mahal, 1989, 20. Print.

______. "Nissim Ezekiel's Humanistic Poetry: An Overview." *The Journal of Indian Writing in English.* 32:2 (July 2004): 3. Print.

Ezekiel, Nissim. *Collected Poems.* New Delhi: O.U.P., 2005, 253. Text.

Iyengar, K.R.S. *Indian Writing in English.* New Delhi: Sterling P., 1985, 657-60. Print.

Jung, Anees. "LSD, The Meaning of Reality: An Interview with Nissim Ezekiel." *The Times of India.* 1 Dec., 1968: 12. Print.

Jussawalla, Adil. *New Poetry, Reading in Commonwealth Literature.* Ed. William Walsh, 1973, 79. Print.

Khanna, Meeta. "Critical Tenets of Nissim Ezekiel's Poetry: A Perspective." *International Journal of English Language, Literature and Humanities.* (September 2015): 594. Print.

Kher, Inder Nath. "Introduction". *Journals on South Asian Literature* 11.3-4, 3-7. Print.

Kurup, P.K.J. *Contemporary Indian Poetry in English.* New Delhi: Atlantic Publishers and Distributors, 1991. 35. Print.

Madge, V.M. "Pride and Prejudice in Ezekiel's Poetry". *Makers of Indian English Literature.* Ed. C.D. Narasimhaiah. Delhi: Pencraft International, 2003, 188-92. Print.

Mohanty, Niranjan. "Self within Self: A Study in the Poetry of Nissim Ezekiel". *Nissim Ezekiel: Dimensions of a Poetic Genius*. Ed. Surya Nath Pandey. Delhi: Doaba House, 1999, 91. Print.

Pastapure, Dileep. "Indianness in Ezekiel's Hymns in Darkness." *Galaxy: International Multidisciplinary Journal*. 3.2 (May 2013): 1. Web. 24 May 2016.

Patil, Suresh Pandurang. "Nissim Ezekiel: A Poet of Social Conscience." *Galaxy: International Multidisciplinary Research Journal*. 2.1 (April 2012): 1. Print.

Prasad, G.J.V. "Always in the Poet's Eye: Nissim Ezekiel's India". *Nissim Ezekiel Remembered*. Ed. Havovi Anklesaria. New Delhi: Sahitya Akademi, 2008, 499. Print.

Varma, Urmila. *Essays on Nissim Ezekiel*. Ed. T.R. Sharma. Meerut: Shalabh, 1994, 170. Print.

Wesly, John, and Chandra, N.D.R. Cultural Complexity in Nissim Ezekiel's Works. *The Criterion: An International Journal in English* 3.3 (September 2012): 13. Web. 24 April 2016.

Select Bibliography

Primary Sources

Poetical Works

Ezekiel, Nissim. *Collected Poems*. Second Edition, O.U.P., 2005. Text.

_______. *The Exact Name*. Calcutta: Writer's Workshop, 1965. Text.

_______. *Hymns in Darkness*. Delhi: O.U.P., 1976. Text.

_______. *Latter-Day Psalms*. Delhi: O.U.P., 1982. Text.

_______. *Poems included in Journal of South Asian Literature* (Spring-Summer 1976): Text.

_______. *Sixty Poems*. Bombay: Strand Book Shop, 1959. Text.

_______. *The Third*. Bombay: The Strand Book Shop, 1958. Text.

_______. *A Time to Change and Other Poems*. London: Fortune Press, 1952. Text.

_______. *The Unfinished Man*. Calcutta: Writer's Workshop, 1960. Text.

Non-Poetical Works

Books

Ezekiel, Nissim. *Naipaul's India and Mine, New Writing in India*. London: Penguin, 1974. Print.

_______. "What is Indian in Indo-English Poetry." *Critical Responses: Common-Wealth Literature*. Ed. Dept. of English Osmania U., New Delhi: Sterling P., Print.

Articles published in Journals and Newspapers

Ezekiel, Nissim. "Interview with Nissim Ezekiel, by Suresh Kohali." *Mahfil* 8.4 (Winter 1972). Print.

_______. "How a Poem is Written." *The Indian Journal of English Studies* (1975-76). Print.

_______. "A Biographical Sketch." *Journal of South Asian Literature* (Spring-Summer 1976). Print.

_______. "A New Arrival in Indo-Anglian Poetry." *Times Weekly* 29.1 (1971). Print.

_______. "Poetry as Knowledge." *Quest* 76 (May-June 1972). Print.

_______. "Isn't Criticism Subjective." *Times of India*, 28 Dec., 1975. Print.

_______. "Eliot's Language: Thirst and Fear," *Times of India,* 6 April 1989. Print.

_______. "Sri Aurobindo on Poetry." *Times of India,* 22 July 1972. Print.

_______. "K.N. Daruwalla." *Quest* 74 Jan.-Feb., 1972. Print.

_______. "Two Poets: A.K. Ramanujan and K.N. Daruwalla." *The Illustrated Weekly of India.* 18 Jan., 1972. Print.

_______. "Introduction." *Books Abroad* (Autumn 1969): Print.

_______. "An Interview with Nissim Ezekiel." *Selected Prose.* Delhi: Oxford, 1992. Print.

Secondary Sources

Books

Abidi, S.Z.H. *Studies in Indo Anglian Poetry.* Bareilly: Prakash Book Depot, 1978. Print.

Acharya, N. Prabhakar. "Achievement and Failure in Nissim Ezekiel's Poetry." *Perspectives on Nissim Ezekiel.* Ed. S.C. Dwivedi. New Delhi: Kitab Mahal, 1989. Print.

Anklesaria, Havovi. Ed. "Cross-Cultural Encounter in Literature." *Nissim Ezekiel Remembered.* New Delhi: Sahitya Akademi, 2008. Print.

_______. Ed. "A Fragment found among Nissim Ezekiel's papers". *Nissim Ezekiel Remembered.* New Delhi: Sahitya Akademi, 2008. Print.

_______. "Interview with Imtiaz and Anil Dharker." *Nissim Ezekiel Remembered*. New Delhi: Sahitya Akademi, 2008. Print.

Beston, John B. "An Interview with Nissim Ezekiel." *Indian Writing in English*. ed. K.N. Sinha. New Delhi: Heritage, 1979. Print.

Bhatnagar, O.P. *Studies in Indian Poetry in English*. Amravati: Popular Book Centre, 1981. Print.

_______. *Perspectives on Indian Poetry in English*. Amravati: Bajaj P., 1985. Print.

Chindhade, Shirish. *Five Indian English Poets*. New Delhi: Atlantic Publishers and Distributors, 2009. Print.

Clemen, Carl. *Religions of the World*. New Delhi: Cosmo P., 2005. Print.

Daruwalla, Keki N. *Collected Poems 1970-2005*. New Delhi: Penguin Books, 2006. Print.

_______. *Two Decades of Indian Poetry 1960—1980*. New Delhi: Vikas, 1980. Print.

Das, Bijay Kumar. *The Horizon of Nissim Ezekiel's Poetry*. New Delhi: B.K. Publishing Corporation, 1995. Print.

_______. "Imagery in the Poetry of Nissim Ezekiel." *Perspectives on Nissim Ezekiel*. Ed. S.C. Dwivedi. New Delhi: Kitab Mahal, 1989. Print.

_______. *Modern Indo-English Poetry*. Bareilly: Prakash Book Depot, 1982. Print.

Das, Kamala. *Summer in Calcutta*. New Delhi: Everest Press, 1965. Text.

Derozio, H.L.V. *Poems*. Calcutta: OUP, 1980. Print.

Dwivedi, A.N. *Kamala Das and Her Poetry*. New Delhi: Atlantic Publishers and Distributors, 2011. Print.

Dwivedi, S.C. *Perspectives on Nissim Ezekiel*. New Delhi: Kitab Mahal, 1989. Print.

Garman, Michael. "Nissim Ezekiel: Pilgrimage and Myth." *Critical Essays on Indian Writing in English*. Ed. M.K. Naik et al. Dharwar: Karnatak U., 1968. Print.

Gupta, Poonam Rani. *Indianness of Two Indian Poets: Nissim Ezekiel and A.K. Ramanujan*. New Delhi: Kunal Books, 2013. Print.

Iyengar, K.R.S. *Introduction to Indian Writing in English*. Bombay: Asia P. House, 1962. Print.

_______. *Indian Writing in English*. New Delhi: Sterling, 1984. Print.

Joshi, Prakash. "Attitudinal Dichotomy in Nissim Ezekiel's Poetry". *Perspectives on Nissim Ezekiel*. Ed. S.C. Dwivedi. New Delhi: Kitab Mahal, 1989. Print.

Karnani, Chetan. *Nissim Ezekiel*. New Delhi: Arnold Hemingway, 1974. Print.

Khan, Eshanullah. *The Evolution of the Religious and Social Life of Man*. New Delhi:

Bait-At-Hikmat Trust, 1989. Print.

King, Bruce. *Modern Indian Poetry in English*. Delhi: OUP, 1987. Print.

_______. *Three Indian Poets*. Madras: Oxford, 1991. Print.

Kumar, Satish. *A Survey of Indian English Poetry*. Bareilly: Prakash Book Depot, 2001. Print.

Kurup, P.K.J. *Contemporary Indian Poetry in English*. New Delhi: Atlantic Publishers and Distributors, 1991. Print.

Lal, P. *Modern Indian Poetry in English*. Calcutta: Writers Workshop, 1969, i-xliv. Print.

Madge, V.M. "Pride and Prejudice in Ezekiel's Poetry". *Makers of Indian English Literature*. Ed. C.D. Narasimhaiah. Delhi: Pencraft International, 2003. Print.

Mahan, Shaila. *The Poetry of Nissim Ezekiel*. Jaipur: Classic P., 2001. Print.

Mahapatra, Jayant. *The Lie of Dawns Poems 1974-2008*. New Delhi: Authors Press, 2009. Print.

Mishra, Rajendra Nath. "Post-Independence Anguish in Nissim Ezekiel's Poetry." *Contemporary Indian Literature in English, A Humanistic Perspective*. Ed. Mithilesh K. Pandey. New Delhi: Kalyani P., 1999. Print.

Mishra, Sanjit. *The Poetic Art of Nissim Ezekiel.* New Delhi: Atlantic Publishers and Distributors, 2001. Print.

Mokashi-Punekar, Shankar. *Theoretical and Practical Studies in Indo-English Literature.* Dharwad: Karnatak U., 1978. Print.

Molloy, Michael. *Experiencing the World's Religions: Tradition, Challenge, and Change.* California: Mayfield P. Company, 1999. Print.

Naik, M.K. "The Ashoka Pillar: Independence and After." *A History of Indian English Literature.* New Delhi: Sahitya Akademi, 1994. Print.

_______. *Aspects of Indian Writing in English.* New Delhi: Macmillan, 2004. Print.

_______. "The Indianness of Indian Poetry in English." *Indian Poetry in English.* ed. H.M. Prasad. Aurangabad: Parimal P., 1983. Print.

_______. "The Tale is in the Sting." *Dimension of Indian English Literature.* New Delhi: Sterling, 1984. Print.

Nandy, Pritish, Ed. *Indian Poetry in English Today.* New Delhi: Sterling Paperbacks, 1973. Print.

Narasimhaiah, C.D. *The Swan and the Eagle.* Shimla: Indian Institute of Advanced Study, 1969. Print.

Nehru, Jawaharlal. *The Discovery of India.* New Delhi: Jawaharlal Nehru Memorial Fund and O.U.P., 1958. Print.

Pal, K.S. *Ramanujan-Ezekiel: Comparative Study.* Nakodar: Aastha P., 1981. Print.

Paranjape, Makarand. *Indian Poetry in English.* Madras: Macmillan, 1993. Print.

Parthasarathy, R. *Ten Twentieth-Century Indian Poets.* New Delhi: O.U.P., 1976. Print.

Peerandina, S. *Contemporary Indian Poetry in English.* Delhi: O.U.P., 1972. Print.

Patel, Gieve. "Introduction" *Nissim Ezekiel: Collected Poems.* O.U.P., 1989. Print.

Prasad, G.J.V. "Always in the Poet's Eye: Nissim Ezekiel's India." *Nissim Ezekiel Remembered.* Ed. Havovi Anklesaria. New Delhi: Sahitya Akademi, 2008. Print.

Prem, P.C.K. *English Poetry in India: A Comprehensive Survey of Trends and Thought Patterns*. Delhi: Authors Press, 2011. Print.

Rahman, Anisur. *Form And Value in the Poetry of Nissim Ezekiel*. New Delhi: Abhinav P., 1981. Print.

Ramamurthi, K.S. *Twenty-Five Indian Poets in English*. New Delhi: Macmillan. Print.

Ramanujan, A.K. *Collected Poems*. Delhi: OUP, 1997. Text.

Ramkrishnan, E.V. "My Background Place is Where I am: The Public Voice in Nissim Ezekiel's Poetry." *Nissim Ezekiel Remembered*. Ed. Havovi Anklesaria. New Delhi: Sahitya Akademi, 2008. Print.

Rao, K. Raghavendra. "The Alienation Games: The Poetry of Nissim Ezekiel." *Perspectives on Indian Poetry in English*. Ed. M.K. Naik. New Delhi: Abhinav, 1984. Print.

Saha, S.C. "Nissim Ezekiel's Contribution to Indian English Poetry". *Contemporary Indian Literature in English: A Humanistic Perspective*. Ed. Mithilesh K. Pandey. New Delhi: Kalyani P, 1999. Print.

Shahane, V.A. "The Religious Philosophical Strain in Nissim Ezekiel's Poetry." *Perspective on Nissim Ezekiel*. Ed. S.C. Dwivedi. Allahabad: K.M. Agencies 1989. Print.

Sharma, Sushil Kumar. "Fourteen Questions to Nissim Ezekiel." *Essays on Nissim Ezekiel*. Ed. T.R. Sharma. Meerut: Shalabh Prakashan, 1994. Print.

Singh, K.K. *Indian English Poetry After Independence*. Jaipur: Book Enclave, 2006. Print.

Taranath, Rajeev and Belliappa, Meena. *The Poetry of Nissim Ezekiel*. Calcutta: Writers' Workshop, 1966. Print.

Thakur, Guruprasad. "Reflection on Ezekiel's "Night of the Scorpion". *Perspectives on Nissim Ezekiel*. Ed. S.C. Dwivedi. New Delhi: Kitab Mahal, 1989. Print.

The New International Webster's Comprehensive Dictionary of the English Language. Encyclopedic Edition. Naples Florida: Trident Press International, 2004. Print.

Tilak, Raghukul. *New Indian English Poets and Poetry*. New Delhi: Rama Brothers, 1995. Print.

Varma, Urmila. *Essays on Nissim Ezekiel.* Ed. T.R. Sharma, Meerut: Shalabh, 1994. Print.

Verghese, C. Paul. *Problems of the Indian Creative Writer in English.* Bombay: Somaiya P., 1971. Print.

Articles, Interviews, and Essays

Acharya, N.P. "Achievement and Failure in Nissim Ezekiel." *The Journal of Indian Writing in English* (July 1986): Print.

Antony, Omana. "Indianism in Nissim Ezekiel: A Study of Night of the Scorpion, The Professor and The Patriot." *Litsearch* 2.2 (June 2012): Print.

Das, Kamala. "I have Lived Beautifully." *Debonair* 5.3 (15 May 1974): Print.

De Souza, Eunice. "Interview with Four Indian English Poets, 1989. *The Bombay Review* 1989: Print.

Deshraj, Anupama, D. "Ingenuity and Indianness in the Works of Jayanta Mahapatra and Arun Kolatkar." *The Criterion: An International Journal in English* 4.3 (Dec., 2012): Web. 21 June 2016.

Garman, Michael. "Nissim Ezekiel: Pilgrimage and Myth." *Journal of South Asian Literature* (Spring-Summer 1976): Print.

Gupta, Ramesh Kumar. "A.K. Ramanujan: A Poet Par-Excellence." Ed. Basavaraj Naikar. *Indian English Literature* 3 (2002): Print.

Harrex, S.C. "Small Scale Reflection on Indian English Language Poetry." *The Journal of Indian Writing in English* (Jan.-July 1980): Print.

Hess, Linda. "Post-Independence Indian Poetry in English." *Quest.* Bombay 49 Spring 1966: Print.

Jung, Anees. "LSD, Meaning of Reality: An Interview with Nissim Ezekiel." *The Times of India* Dec. 1968: Print.

Jussawalla, Adil. "The New Poetry." *Journal of Commonwealth Literature* (1968): Print.

Khanna, Meeta. "Critical Tenets of Nissim Ezekiel's Poetry: A Perspective." *International Journal of English Language, Literature and Humanities* (Sept. 2015): Print.

Kher, Inder Nath. "Introduction". *Journals on South Asian Literature* 11.3-4 (1976): Print.

McCutchion, David. "Examen de Midi," *The Miscellany* 29 (Oct. 1968): Print.

Naik, M.K. "Landscapes and Inscapes." *Kavya Bharti* 1 (1988): Print.

Pastapure, Dileep. "Indianness in Ezekiel's Hymns in Darkness." *Galaxy: International Multidisciplinary Journal* 3.2 (May 2013): Web. 24 May 2016.

Patil, J. Birje. "Interior Cadences: The Poetry of Nissim Ezekiel." *The Literary Criterion* (1976): Print.

Patil, Suresh Pandurang. "Nissim Ezekiel: A Poet of Social Conscience." *Galaxy: International Multidisciplinary Research Journal* 2.1 (April 2012): Print.

Pinto, Jerry. *Mid Day Multimedia* 10 Jan. 2004: n. pag. Web. 15 Feb. 2016.

Rana, Sunita. "A Study of Indian English Poetry." *International Journal of Scientific and Research Publications* 10.2 (10 Oct. 2012): Web. 15 June 2016. (www.ijsrp.org)

Shahane, V.A. "The Religious-Philosophical Strain in Nissim Ezekiel's Poetry." *Journal of South Asian Literature* (1976): Print.

Sharma, Mukul Kumar, Sharma, Kapil, and Mishra, Sanjit. "The Marginalized Women in Jayanta Mahapatra's Poetry." *International Journal of English and Education* 3.2 (July 2013): Web. 21 June 2016.

Verma, K.D. "Myth and Imagery in The Unfinished Man: A Critical Reading." *Journals of South Asian Literature.* 11.3-4 (Spring-Summer 1976): Print.

Verma, Priti. "Crisis and Redemption: Therapeutic Canvas of Nissim Ezekiel's Poetry." *The Indian Journal of English Studies* XLIV (2007): Print.

Walsh, William. "Two Indian Poets." *The Literary Criterion.* 3.11 (Winter 1974): Print.

Wesly, John, and Chandra, N.D.R. "Cultural Complexity in Nissim Ezekiel's Works." *The Criterion: An International Journal in English* 3.3 (Sept. 2012): Print.

Index